Acknowledgements

Where does one begin? My late parents, Isidore and Esther, ought to be the first to be thanked, for creating in the midst of all their challenges, a warm little nurturing family nest. Here we felt loved and cared for. Here we were encouraged to learn and to look forward to a boundless future. Here we were given a double dose of pride - pride as Jews and pride as Americans.

To our teachers, both in the public schools and ethnic after-hours schools, who gave far more than they were paid to, the tools of thinking, expressing and creating, I owe a boundless debt.

To my son Kees, a very special acknowledgement is due - without him this book simply could not have happened.

To my creative partner, designer Victor DiPace, I especially owe thanks for taking the mess of text and pictures and turning it into a readable work of art.

I wish to thank all who shared their photos with me to help new generations visualize what life was truly like in this unusual community -- and to preserve it in coherent fashion for scholars of the 21st century and beyond.

BROWNSVILLE: THE JEWISH YEARS

Celebrating Hope, Hard Work, Tolerance and the Triumph of the Human Spirit

By Sylvia Siegel Schildt

Cover design and book graphics by
Victor DiPace

Copyright Library of Congress September 2007
ISBN Number 1-4196-8386-1

Published by BookSurge

Introductory Remarks

This is not the first book about Brownsville. Others have been written by scholars and social activists. Each one has had a specific focus - from the role of women to the racial crises of the Sixties. My previous book was a nostalgic collection of vignettes of life as lived by young children and it was written in both Yiddish and English, in the moment, entirely in the present tense, without reference to our time at all, without any judgmental observations. It was a limited edition, published by the International Association of Yiddish Clubs, meant mostly for speakers and students of Yiddish.

I have set myself a totally different task here. And it is not a simple one. My goal is to re-create Brownsville as we lived it, layer by layer. I know going in that it will be warmly received by most who lived the experience. I even suspect it will be of interest to those who are curious about the day to day life of an urban immigrant community.

But what I really hope to achieve is to give those who have had a totally different experience, a taste of what it was like to grow up Jewish in Brownsville, when great events took over the nation and the world, show how we coped and transcended our challenges - and to be able to extract from it some insights that are relative to life in the very different 21st century.

This is a typical Brownsville street scene with stickball game in progress. Players and pedestrians seem oblivious of each other. The elevated train in the deep background tells me this scene looks towards Livonia Avenue. Neighbors sit outside to cool off, watch the action or to socialize.

But I want to do more than that. I want to reach out to those who have few points of relevance to start out with, the younger generations, especially the Jewish-American kids of today, and help them understand their most recent history, what they came out of, how their grandparents and great-grandparents transcended difficulties to build for them the life of affluence they enjoy today and probably take for granted.

I have tried to enrich the book with archival and personal photos, supplemented with highly personal commentaries. It is my hope that the cumulative effect of these photos will add up to a highly evocative texture that enriches the text itself.

The book is meant to be a first-hand account and is therefore limited in the main to the period in which I experienced Brownsville first-hand - the Thirties, Forties and part of the Fifties. During this period, Brownsville was a Jewish world, densely populated, economically challenged, with one foot in the past, the other stepping eagerly into the beckoning arms of American culture.

The Jewish layer of settlement began in the late Nineteenth Century and just about ended in the late Fifties and Early Sixties. Then it was the turn of African Americans, followed Puerto Ricans, then people from Central America. These peoples, as were the Jewish residents before them, were the poorest of the poor. I will try to carry the reader into the Brownsville I knew and show how the main events of our lifetime, the Depression, the two World Wars, the Holocaust, the post-war Boom and the Cold War played into the lives of Brownsville's residents.

Recently, something new has been added - I read that Brownsville is undergoing gentrification and middle class private housing is replacing tenements and projects. Probably all to the good. Being poor is no great honor.

But I believe it would be a mistake to obliterate all traces of the Brownsville I knew, which taught us bitter lessons and shaped our values, and helped us carry the American dream forward into the future.

Sylvia Schildt
September, 2007

The parking lot on East New York Avenue, circa the 20's. By our time, it had gone downhill and was full of tires and junk. It was situated between Amboy and Herzl Streets, seen here. Adjacent to the parking lot on Herzl was Ruderman's candy store, a kids' hangout spot, also site of the only telephone most people had. Corner Herzl and East New York was a grocery. When our father was not working, the grocer recorded our purchases in a little book. He got paid back little by little when work picked up.

Most of what I see here is memory, in my mind's eye. Across the street was the shul; it's an open space now. Inside the building, in the middle opening, is a courtyard that goes below street level. I can discern where our kitchen window was located. Our mother used to sit on a little homemade outcropping when she washed the outside of the windows. Her legs dangled above the kitchen floor and the sight scared us half to death. Seems like many windows are boarded up, but people still live here; I can tell by the clothes hanging out to dry. Behind, are the "new" projects.

Oh, the wonders of 21st century technology. I am able to locate a birds eye view of the Brownsville street on which I spent my first seventeen years. Even the house I grew up in. It is the only original building left on my block, Herzl Street corner Pitkin Avenue. With my cursor, I take a slow "helicopter" ride along the adjacent streets and see how the housing projects have replaced the derelict tenement buildings, straining to discern from the aerial view of today's Brownsville, the Brownsville that was.

I am able to make out my house. Unbelievable. Like a trip back in time.

It's so small in the scheme of things. It was once my entire universe and that of my three brothers, sister and parents. The terrain on the side streets has totally changed. But the Pitkin Avenue buildings survive, not with the fancy stores they once housed, but stores nonetheless, meeting the needs of the current wave of residents.

As I look at each window of my old apartment building, despite its changes, I can re-capture the 38 Herzl Street I knew. I see the columned doorway which opened into the small outer hallway. There used to be a radiator there, a big one, which, on snow-strewn winter days, after we had built forts or enjoyed snowball fights, served as a dryer for our mittens. The smell of charring wool was wonderful - of course the mittens never dried. And we would put the hot damp things back on and go out to play after we had warmed up a bit.

Mrs. Becker, the super's wife, would scold us for messing up the hallway she had just mopped hours ago, which we were now soiling with galoshes, snow, slush and dirty footprints. To be fair, I must say, she also included her own grandchildren in the scolding.

I remember sitting on the front steps on summer evenings after supper, reading until the archway light proved too dim. I read Jane Eyre there for the first time when I was in Junior High and cried bitter tears for the young Jane so mistreated by fate and Aunt Reed.

I see the sidewalk where the girls played "A, My Name Is Anna". The surrounding projects have disrupted the clear flow of street where the boys played stickball, dodging cars between swings.

We played school with the running boards of parked cars serving as a classroom for four kids.

Stickball, the game of choice on Brownsville streets.

Tante Brokhe looks out at me from her second floor front apartment with her sad, wise-as-Solomon eyes. She never learned to read, never became a citizen, but was a proud American, and Roosevelt's picture in the form of a gold-fringed banner, hung proudly in her kitchen. She and her husband Moishe Rosenblatt, owned a fish store on Blake Avenue, which offered live fish in a tank, which they killed and scaled and chopped into smaller wrappable pieces. They both worked in the store and had no children of their own. Their numerous nieces and nephews in the Bronx came to visit on the occasional weekend or holidays. She and my mother were very close and with our real grandparents in Europe, their fate uncertain, she served as an honorary grandmother. She used to let me polish the huge dining room table, especially the carved twisted legs, which I considered a treat. To this day I love the smell of lemon oil furniture polish.

The budding Siegel family, posing on Tar Beach, the rooftop of 38 Herzl Street.
Father Izzy holds Leibl, mother Esther holds Elliot, I stand in front.

Every new dress, every new suit, any good report card, meant a visit upstairs to show it off to Tante Brokhe. If you got a new pocketbook to go with your outfit, it meant a shiny quarter as "good luck money"to put in it. And when caring for five fighting youngsters trapped indoors on a rainy or stormy day, brought my poor mother to her wits end, Tante Brokhe's second floor apartment became a children's sanctuary and a place for mother to calm down.

Our mother always shared her special dishes with Tante Brokhe and Uncle Moishe, as well as with the super's daughter Tessie and her handsome Irish husband Jack Hart. They lived on the third floor above us and Jack loved my mother's cholent stew no end. When these delectable dishes were cooked, it would often be my job to climb the stairs, ring the doorbells and deliver them mother's gift -- a steaming hot plate wrapped in foil.

Below the Rosenblatts, lived the Beckers, our supers from Austria, she with light brown hair, combed, tightly-twisted braids placed like a crown on top of her head. Mrs. Becker was the one who scrubbed the steps and hallways at least once a week, using a strong-smelling green soap and scrub brush. I have lived many places since Herzl Street, but Mr. Becker's daily garbage pick-up at our apartment door, was the best service I have ever known. Every day but Sundays, Christmas and Easter, at about 4 pm, the doorbell would ring and there would be his smiling face, cap on head, pipe in mouth. He would take out the trash and put it in a larger container in the dumbwaiter between our two apartments, and pull on the rope, lowering the trash to the cellar.

Mrs. Becker was a constant crocheter and their apartment was filled with crocheted lacy doilies, towels, many of them with messages in German.

We celebrated all the Jewish holidays, but the Beckers'and Harts lights, trees and decorations gave us a sneak taste of Christmas as well.

Generally, the relations between the Siegels, us, and the Becker's and Hart's, were neighborly and cordial. My brother Leibl and their son Ritchie Hart were lifelong friends from toddlerhood on, until Ritchie died of cancer decades later. I was friendly with their eldest daughter Lizzie, until I moved away. But I noticed that when Jewish people came to visit, Mommie offered tea and cake. But when non-Jews like Jack Hart came calling, she brought out the schnapps.

Besides school with its inevitable homework, and Jewish school, also with homework, Brownsville's kids were never at a loss for something to do. The street itself was a playground with games like Hit the Penny, Ringolevio. We reveled in spaldeens, jacks and jump ropes, riding bikes, skates, scooters made from crates. We jumped sidewalk cracks and played potsey. We collected and traded the insides of Dixie cups, Popsicle sticks, and baseball cards, especially those with Dodgers baseball players on them. We sent away for prizes from radio programs.

We made toys out of soda bottle caps, high-bouncing balls out of rubber bands, turned discarded boxes into dollhouses, sold lemonade and used comic books to each other. My brother saved up for a silent movie projector and showed Betty Boop cartoons and Three Stooges in our tiny kitchen, for a tiny admission fee. We called it the Loew's Siegel.

And if while playing Hit the Penny, a kid dropped a coin down the grate, there was no need for tears. All you had to do was attach a wad of well-chewed gum to a string, lower it until it caught the coin, and then you pulled it up.

The fine art of fetching what you dropped in the sewer - a ball, a half-eaten candy bar.

Public spaces abounded - Betsy Head Park meant ballgames, checkers and huge pool for hundreds.

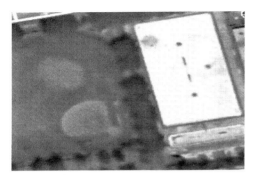

The pool still stands. As does the diving pool. The pool was huge, with stone bleachers around it for sitting, sunning, picnicking.

At Lincoln Terrace Park on Eastern Parkway, you could play tennis for free, use the swings, slides and seesaws or have a picnic on the grass.

Our father used to play cards there with friends during summer slack seasons, and if we found him enjoying a winning streak, he was always good for a quarter or two that could be turned into cokes, ice creams or Crackerjacks at the kiosk.

Saturdays and some holidays were movie days. It was an all-day affair, beginning when the doors opened, until the matrons chased the kids out at around five or six. You brought food from home as well as spending money for drinks, candy and popcorn. Kiddie matinees featured cartoons, action-packed serials (today's blockbusters in my view are little more than those serials, souped up with high tech special effects), news of the day, short subjects and two features. Often they were the same movies the grown-ups saw, sometimes different.

Jewish holidays meant getting all dressed up with no place to go, if your parents were observant. You couldn't carry money, play ball or other street games, ride a bike or take public transportation. If your parents were more liberal, you had fewer limitations and could go to the movies, but many of the stores would be closed. Outward violations of holiday no-nos were out, out of respect for the religious in the community, so especially on the most religious holiday days like Rosh Hashonah and Yom Kippur, groups of kids with no coins in their pockets, but dressed in their best, would stroll up and down Pitkin Avenue, all the way to the Parks and along Eastern Parkway. We would dart in and out of the many shuls - some of them had full choirs and well-known cantors. For some of us, it was a form of entertainment, for others, the commanded practice of their religion. Watching people in their finery was also part of the Jewish holiday experience.

Decaying remains of a typical Browsville shul, not very impressive, wedged in between tenements and apartment houses. The men davened (prayed) downstairs and the women upstairs. They were packed on High Holy Days when famous cantors sang there.

Meat stores came in only one flavor - kosher -- until the advent of the supermarket. You had a personal relationship with your butcher who would promise to save you the best cuts for your money.

But inside the homes, you savored the traditional holiday dishes, from Passover seders to blintzes and sour cream on Shevuos, the candles, the noisy come and go of relatives.

And of course, on these days, Jewish kids had no school at all, which made them the envy of their non-Jewish classmates who had to attend. The handful of non-Jewish students in the schools attended do-nothing classes with a handful of do-nothing teachers. I always felt it was unfair.

Feeding and clothing a family of our size was no mean task. Mother was a formidable bargainer on Belmont Avenue. Between them, they made many of our clothing items. And the younger kids got the hand-me-downs of the older ones.

Bargaining was the norm for pushcart shoppers of Belmont Avenue, not only at the pushcarts that sold produce and sundries, but in the stores that lined these packed streets. The language of commerce was Yiddish, or some form of it.

And sometimes, for a treat, we got the hand-me-downs of our Basson relations from the Bronx. When we were old enough to travel on our own, we would take the subway from Brownsville in Brooklyn to our great-aunt Esther's grand apartment on the Grand Concourse in the Bronx, be served a chic Americanized lunch (very skimpy by our standards) and then carry home by subway some bags of hand-me-down clothes. My cousin Lois, Tante Esther's granddaughter, although younger, was taller, so her clothes worked well for me. One such garment was a navy and white checked spring coat with a little white collar and navy piping - the skirt swung out a little and felt very princess-y. I loved that coat. My mother, who had a passion for accessorizing, bought me red patent shoes, gloves and a wide brimmed sailor hat. I wore it when I was reciting the

Passover Seder Hagaddah in Yiddish with my Jewish school classmates at a venue no less elegant than the Waldorf-Astoria. That was my Passover outfit that year. I cried when, after two or three seasons, I outgrew that coat.

In recent years, I rediscovered my cousin Lois and we exchange e-mails. I have tried to explain to her the value of the coat to me and why it still shines in my memory.

Brownsville Boys Club was a self-governing group that provided play and growth opportunities for Brownsville youth.

Pitkin Avenue: The Heart of Brownsville

This is Pitkin Avenue in the glory days, packed with well-dressed shoppers and baby carriages. I make this out to be late Forties or early Fifties because of the parking meters. Looks like the weekend crowds. Street vendor is plying his trade. Shops attracted locals and people from as far away as Long Island and the Bronx.

How do you begin to describe Pitkin Avenue as it was in the 30's, 40's and 50's, the height of Brownsville's Golden Age?

It was a thriving thoroughfare, filled with a huge diversity of shops on both sides of the avenue, chain stores like Woolworths, mom and pops, even a stand, Jungle Jim's, that sold pineapple coconut drinks called pina coladas and coconut slices in a cup of water. The owner sported a pith helmet and a Yiddish accent. This stand, in sharp contrast to the poverty and slum dwellings that surrounded it, was also an incongruity alongside the fancy shops, since it was surrounded with green paper fringe that looked like grass. Pitkin Avenue prided itself on top of the line stores. Shoppers flocked from as far as Long Island and the Bronx to check out the men's custom clothiers and haberdashery shops, women's fashion stores, places where you could have a suit made for your Bar Mitzvah boy or equally quickly, an Easter Communion outfit. For bargains you went to the pushcarts and side stores of Belmont Avenue.

On a busy Sunday afternoon, Pitkin Avenue's sidewalks were jam-packed with ladies wheeling baby carriages and kiddie strollers, men in suits, ties and fedoras and boys in bomber jackets and dungarees, gum-chewing girls in sweaters, skirts and walking shoes with bobby socks. The women wore hats. No respectable woman left even the seediest cold water flat without a hat. Many baby carriages wore a big bow at the back of the hood, indicating the sex of the prize baby within. Other baby carriages doubled as shopping carts, while toddlers held on to the carriage bars under Mom's watchful eyes.

Weaving in among the crowds were street vendors, blind beggars who sang gospel hymns and handers-out of political flyers and advertisements of every description. Often these handers-out would engage in heated discussions with people on the street. If the subject got too heated, a crowd might gather, and a sidewalk pedestrian bottleneck would develop.

You could tell the season by what the street-sellers offered. Some bore their wares on a tray strapped on to their bodies - sesame brittle and halvah were sold that way. The coming of fall meant the arrival of those metal carts with built-in ovens, shlepped by one or another weary individual. You could smell the delicious aromas of roasted chestnuts or sweet potatoes and know what time of the year it was. Fall. Other times you could get franks with sauerkraut, mustard and relish, hot potato knishes, or roasted peanuts in a bag, and that heavenly treat for a nickel, the charlotte russe.

Ah, the charlotte russe. It was a round of pound cake, maybe an inch thick, seated in a white paper cup shape, surrounded with fluted paper sides and filled to overflowing with whipped cream that swirled to a peak. And gleaming on top of the whipped cream point perched a maraschino cherry. Pure bliss. Impossible to eat without getting at least a dot of whipped cream on your nose.

Many of the stores along Pitkin Avenue stayed open year-round. But the fashion stores that sold dresses, stylish coats and suits, sportswear, shoes and millinery would shut up shop after the last clearances in July, soap up the windows and go on vacation. Literally. On the front door would be a hand-painted sign saying - "Closed for Vacation - Back on or about August 15th."

On or about August 15th the new fall fashion scene would arrive. For those of us who cared about fashion, that August 15th time was the signal to discover the new trends, styles, skirt lengths and colors. Fake fall foliage and acorns would appear on the windows, anchored by staple guns and tape and ta-da - the fashion show would begin. Mannequins were set up, duly accessorized, and the windows, shops and streets would come alive again. Many were pedestrians from the neighborhood; others parked their cars in nearby outdoor parking lots, along Pitkin Avenue or on the crowded side streets, which had the nasty effect of interrupting stick ball games and other children's activities. Others came by subway and bus.

Clever collusion abounded. One shoe shop called Triebitz, sold less stylish corrective footwear, often prescribed by foot doctors, called chiropodists. And conveniently upstairs, above the shoe shop, was a chiropodist to prescribe this footwear.

My mother bought her good walking shoes at this establishment at street level and saw her chiropodist upstairs. The shoes were ugly, but she swore by their comfort.

One store, corner Herzl and Pitkin, was a shop where you could have corsets and bras made to order. You could see the sewing women from the street with their white or pinkish brocades and matching yarns, working away. Fittings were in private. My mother was of the decided opinion that you could not be well-dressed above, without a good foundation underneath. Changing times brought an end to constricting corsets and the site was replaced by a Barton's chocolate store which on Passover sold chocolate-covered matzos.

This also of course coincided with back-to-school, so the shoe stores and stationery stores that sold school supplies became crowd scenes. On the first day of school, each child took home a list of must-haves - loose-leaf notebooks, composition books, shiny book covers to protect the textbooks teachers would hand out, pens, pencils, gum and ink erasers, tab dividers, manila folders and envelopes, paper clips, rubber bands, inks, art supplies and a host of items that would send financially-pressed parents into tailspins. But they managed, because if there was one thing Brownsville knew, it was that school was important.

There were stores that specialized in books and records. From these, blared forth operatic favorites, Yiddish tunes or the latest in popular music. Some stores sold radios and phonographs and when TV sets appeared after the War, store windows became living displays of TV sets, by which pedestrians who had not yet crossed the line into TV ownership, could be wooed. Sometimes all you could see were test patterns. Other times, especially into the Fifties, the Dodgers games were on display to gather potential customers. You could, in those days, walk along Pitkin Avenue, and between radio and TV blaring from these stores, catch all the baseball action without missing a beat. And when there was a big game on, one which might seal the pennant for the Dodgers, crowds would gather.

TV was such a hot ticket, that those who did not yet own a set would gather in the tiny, crowded living rooms of those who did, just to watch their favorite programs.

Abe Stark wore several hats - merchant, philanthropist and savvy politician who eventually became Brooklyn Borough President. Here he is handing out tickets for an Ebbetts Field Dodgers game to a group of boys, in front of his Pitkin Avenue emporium.

Several famous haberdashers also did business along Pitkin Avenue, the two most famous being Jack Diamond and Abe Stark. I remember Jack Diamond, because I was playing in front of that store early one April evening, when I learned that FDR had died. The other, because Abe Stark wore three hats, one as merchant, the other as community activist and the third as politician - he eventually became the Borough President of Brooklyn. Another famous haberdasher in Kansas City also went into politics, but unlike Abe Stark, he left retail - that was Harry Truman. Haberdasheries sold shirts, ties, fancy socks, tie clips and cuff links and you went there when it was time to buy a gift for hard-working dads.

There were stores that sold almost nothing but ladies stockings in very subtly differentiated shades of beige. Plus some black, worn by Italian widows and white, worn by nurses.

You could buy figs and imported candies on Pitkin Avenue. Or a pound of sliced tongue at Shapiro's Delicatessen. Or foot long hot dogs at the Kishke King on Pitkin and Tapscott. Or sip a malted at the Chocolate Shoppe between Herzl and Strauss. The luncheonette on the corner of Strauss and Pitkin was called Haddon Hall because its cigar sign was the biggest sign visible outside the premises - this was the home of both the egg cream and the lime rickey and the year-round source for charlotte russes. Haddon Hall featured sit-down munching for weary pedestrians and even juke boxes to keep you entertained.

In the mood for "chinks"? Pitkin Avenue had you covered. Chinks was the local name for Chinese food, mainly chop suey, meals. You didn't go out for a Chinese meal, you went to "eat chinks." Upstairs at the Wu Han Tea Gardens, you sampled one from column A and one from column B. At Hoffman's Cafeteria, a steaming table offered all the favorites of a Jewish style eatery, from knishes, kugels and stuffed cabbage to huge deli sandwiches. It was popular with unattached males in the neighborhood and consequently a source of customers for local ladies of the evening. At least, so I heard.

There were banks on Pitkin Avenue as well as branch offices of Brooklyn Union Gas and Consolidated Ed, so you could make savings, withdrawals and even pay your utility bills right there on the avenue. You could sweat away impurities at the Turkish baths, a favorite with Russian-born immigrants.

You could see the latest movies, fresh from Broadway, in kitchy luxury at the Loew's Pitkin, or second run B-pictures at the Stadium on Chester, just around the corner from Pitkin. This was the best place to watch Charlie Chan movies and mystery potboilers. If you had a yen for foreign movies, including Russian propaganda works, you could catch them at the Hopkinson, formerly a Yiddish theater.

Pitkin Avenue strollers across the street from Loew's Pitkin. Note, the men are wearing hats too, not just women and girls.

If you were Jewish, you could even get married on Pitkin Avenue. Several catering establishments flourished, offering sit-down dinners with dancing to follow for a gown and tuxedo clad guest list. Klezmer bands furnished the music after the ceremony, with everything from Yiddish and Hebrew melodies to the latest in pops and patriotic tunes. And it always, always ended with the playing of "Good night, sweetheart", after which the musicians would pack up their heavy instruments and shlep to the Pitkin Ave. bus stop, dragging their baggage home on the subway.

Several florist shops, little backdoor places like Aks's florists, and the long-lived Hyman Spitz saw to it that the bouquets arrived on time and as ordered. And Paulette Studios took the pictures. In the earlier years, photographic plates of the wedding pictures were spread out on the sidewalk to mature in the sunlight.

Hyman Spitz Florists once catered the floral arrangements for the finest weddings, bar mitzvahs and other occasions, now an object of interest for urban archeologists

The glitz, glitter and throbbing pace of Pitkin Avenue was concentrated from Stone Avenue in one direction and fed into the triangle shaped Zion Memorial Park, just past the Loew's Pitkin, becoming Eastern Parkway on the other.

This Zion Memorial Park was built in memory of Jewish War Veterans of WWI, and was the finishing point of patriotic parades at which local and national figures spoke. It was also a place to play chess and cards, and a flirtation spot, which earned it the nickname of Kitzl Park, "tickle" park.

And did Pitkin Avenue love a parade. There were many - every holiday was an excuse - and during the war it was used also to highlight war bond drives and similar events. During election times, candidates both local and national would stage parades, equipped also with trucks that blared out their message.

But that's not all there was to Pitkin Avenue - it came in layers. Its already old three storey buildings housed second floor businesses as well, many with avenue frontage and signs - clothiers, tailors shops, apartments for rent, doctors and dentists offices, specimen labs for doctors and hospitals, and even political headquarters representing not only Democrats and Republicans, but also the influential New York State Liberal Party, the Communist Party and the American Labor and Progressive parties. Pitkin Avenue was an ever-changing scene, reflecting the seasons, each with its own peculiar sights, sounds and smells.

Pitkin Avenue was treated with respect in Brownsville. You dressed up when you went for a walk. Sunday and holiday promenades were family events. Pitkin Avenue shops dutifully observed the main Jewish holidays and closed down, for the most part, sunset to sunset. Its chrome and brass trim were brightly polished and shiny glass storefront surfaces reflected the images and pulse of life in the Brownsville that was.

Major Parade on Pitkin Avenue. The banner reads Pitkin Avenue Merchants Association. I also spot a cafeteria next to the bank. And further down, a corner luncheonette I think I recognize.

Second floor businesses like Shimmies men's clothiers added an additional dimension to the Pitkin Avenue scene. This is Saratoga and Pitkin. Heading towards East New York Avenue is the Western Union. Above, were apartments or storage for the businesses below.

In today's world, he might have been suspected of being some kind of pervert. But in Brownsville, Joe's comings and goings barely caused an eyebrow lift. Except with the kids. He would be a presence up and down the avenue, with his ever-handy little record book, selling cheap little toys to kids on the installment plan. You bought your little wind-up car, toy, coloring book or game, cheaper than at Woolworth's, and you paid him as you could. He wore very thick glasses and his clothes were always rumpled, but he was always surrounded by boys and girls. In his hand, was the little brown book in which he entered your name - he didn't need the address most of the time, since he knew where every kid lived, more or less. As you made your payment, he would lick his pencil point and make the entry, crossing it out when the delicious object had been completely paid for. His strollings did earn him the unofficial title of the Mayor of Pitkin Avenue.

Another young adult male with a somewhat iffy reputation was Bright Eyes and he roamed around with a group my mother called "bums." This was because they seemed to have no steady occupation and spent their daylight hours gambling, going to the track or ballgames, or playing stickball on the street. Bright Eyes also wore thick glasses through which he looked out on the world with a squint. He could be seen leaning against lampposts leering at passing girls. The "bums" ate out a lot. Hoffman's Cafeteria was a popular haunt among the bachelor set, and the sight of loose males, standing around the cafeteria sidewalk, toothpicks dangling from their lips, was very common.

Eventually a number of them joined the services to fight the Nazis or were drafted, thus becoming "de-bummified". One of the crowd, Sonny Levine, married my cousin Dorothy and they wound up running an Indian Trading Post in Albuquerque, New Mexico. He had always had a steady job before the wedding, manning a subway token booth. But Bright Eyes was of course unfit for the service and hardly marriage material. So to the best of my knowledge, he went through life as a sad, alienated creature.

A witch roamed the streets of Brownsville, and I am ashamed to admit that I am one of those who was afraid of her. We kids on the street would run and hide, calling out to all and sundry, "The witch. The witch." She was taller than most women in the neighborhoods, thin and gaunt. I never saw her in any other color than black - black from the little hat she wore over her gray hair, a hat held in place by a black rubber band, to her laced up shoes. Very scary looking. Yet one morning, there she was, sitting at our kitchen table, dipping a Kaiser roll in coffee, chatting softly and amiably with my mother. I can't have been more than five or six years old and later mother told me she was a poor woman and it was a good deed to feed those needier than ourselves. I remember feeling so ashamed of myself, and so proud of my mother.

Our most notable town drunk was a man in his fifties or sixties, who went by the name of "Drunken Stanley" -- he lived in one of the dank, basement apartments on Herzl Street. By nature amiable, he would always greet the kids in his drawling Southern accent. When coherent, he would even exchange general pleasantries. But Stanley was often seen blind, reeling drunk, stumbling along the sidewalk, holding onto the lamppost for support, crashing his liquor bottles on the concrete, and finishing with vomiting and falling to the ground, singing until he passed out.

An interesting side note - just about every family gave charity. No matter how poor the family, every kitchen had a pushke or two (a metal box with sealed coin slot), one in blue and white for the Jewish National Fund, others for various yeshivas, orphanages and homes for the aged. Adults and children were in the habit of dropping in pennies and nickels destined for others less fortunate or for the dream of building a homeland for the Jewish people.

Next to our building, which still stands despite the projects, was a row of tenement brownstones, with cluttered front facing fire escapes, dilapidated front steps and barely livable basement dwellings. None of them exceeded three stories in height, which was a law in Brooklyn (unlike Manhattan) for buildings without elevators. Perhaps that's why trees could grow in Brooklyn. The first of these buildings housed, among others, a mother (we never knew her name) and an unmarried daughter named Dorothy. Kids called her "di meshugene", the crazy one. You never heard her mother's voice, but the daughter's screams, tears, protests and tirades could pierce the silence of a summer afternoon, The scenario was almost always the same - desperate protests that her mother was responsible for her state of spinsterhood and threats to kill her mother "one of these days". Thankfully, this never happened. But the forty-ish woman with dyed back hair was an object of pity and derision on our block.

We had two neighborhood cops on the beat and we knew them by their first names. There was Freddy da cop and Al the policeman. Freddy was a plumpish, graying Italian with bushy eyebrows - I can still remember his voice, which had a little sandpapery roughness to it. And Al, I think he was Irish, looked like a movie set kind of cop. 38 Herzl had a green phone box near the entrance, where the local police would come to make their reports, and there was often conversation between the kids and residents and our regular beat cops. Sometimes a police car would be parked on the sidewalk and Freddy, Al or one of their buddies would use the car seat as a chair, joining in on the neighborhood gossip. It could be there for hours at a time. Sometimes a kid would be allowed to sit in the revered police car and pretend to drive it.

Early one summer afternoon, my little brother Elliot went missing. We looked for him everywhere. He had been downstairs playing, as did all the other kids. Neighbors always kept an eye out for the kids. Where could a four-year old go? Who would want to harm a little boy? Did he get run over, God forbid, by a car? Was he kidnapped by gypsies? Everyone got in on the act - they combed the streets all around Pitkin and East New York Avenue, checked the movie theaters in case he had wandered in, even checked the local parks as far away as Lincoln Terrace Park. It was summer and he had been wearing what was called a polo shirt, a pair of shorts made by our mother, sneakers and socks. Finally we called the cops. Al came when he finished his beat. Freddy came a little later. By now my father had come home and everyone was gathered in front of the house, by the green phone.

Then one of the cops went into the car - and there little Elliot was. Fast asleep in the hollow of the back seat. How did he get there? Well, as he explained, in his quirky Yiddish accent, he wanted to drive the car himself.
"I toined on de key, I toined de veel, pooshed de clutch, and I drrrove avay."

Seems some of the older boys, the ones my mother called "the bums" had thought it funny to teach a four-year old how to drive. He used to regale them with, "You toin on de key, you open de clutch, you toin de veel, and you drrrive avay." Except that after trying for awhile to drive the empty, open police car on a hot summer day, he got tired, felt like a nap, and curled up in a cool corner in the back of the police car.

We also had a variety of colorful vendors who went door to door. One was the "alte zakhn man" the man who traded in old clothes and household goods. He went up and down the streets calling out *"Alte zakhn, alte zakhn."* And he would attract passing housewives, or cause heads to pop out from front-facing windows to summon his attention. He had an old flat-bed truck in which he kept the merchandise which he bought or sold. I remember him in our apartment a few times - our mother would sell him our outgrown clothes or bed linens, a few cents for this, a few cents for that. Literally.

For those who still had iceboxes, rather than refrigerators, and there were several on the third floor of our house, there was Freddy the iceman, a small-statured Sicilian, who would tote big blocks of ice, with a pick, all in a dark canvas sack which he carried on his back, his hands free to grasp the banisters. He loved to sing as he went, and his truck was pulled by a horse - one of the few that remained from the old days.

The least-liked resident of our street was the woman who owned one of the brownstones on our street - Mrs. Foreman. She was a stickler for keeping her halls, steps and sidewalk clean. Her dark, but graying hair was pulled into a tight bun, her face grim. She would stand guard in her doorway, apron-clad, broom in hand, which she worked like a sword of vengeance, with resolute strokes, churning up dust and paper litter. But she also hated kids loitering in front of her house and would chase us with the broom, calling out in her Hungarian-Yiddish accent, *"Go to your own hose."*

Sneaking into the movies or overstaying the matinee periods allotted to kids on weekends, was almost a sport. One of the hardest places to operate in was the Loew's Palace, the second-run theater on Strauss Street corner East New York Avenue, thanks to the dreaded Sally the Matron. She was a middle-aged bleached blonde who wore fancy-rimmed glasses held in place by a cord. Plumpish but tightly corseted, she always wore a white nurses' uniform. This was helpful in the darkened theater.

Summer was the best sneak-in time, because the air conditioning at the Palace often broke down, so the side exit doors were left ajar and the theater was dark. You always came in mid-movie, when all eyes were elsewhere. Out-Sallying Sally was a sport. Summer was also better because there were no coats and hats to worry about - if caught inside, you could always say you were coming from the bathroom.

All the local movies had matrons, especially during kid matinee periods, but she was the most alert, and was known to kick offenders out of the theater. She showed no mercy. She would find your hiding place, flash her flashlight into your eyes, and with her raspy voice, in which you could discern no motherly softness, command you to leave at once, following you out the "door of no return."

Just as Sally of the Palace was a source of irritation, there was another woman who gave great delight to decades of Brownsville's moviegoers, old and young alike - Henrietta Kamern, later billed as Henrietta Cameron, organist-in-residence at the Loew's Pitkin by trade. On the marquee and billboards she was listed simply as "Henrietta at the Organ".

Henrietta Kamern

Henrietta Kamern was a fixture at the organ, adding entertainment value to the moments between showings and also at vaudeville performances, which while dying out after the arrival of talkies, continued intermittently. I saw several of them, the most notable for me, an appearance by Buck and Bubbles.

In these days of multi-plex theaters, it must be hard for people to understand the value of such an individual and the role she played. Originally, the Pitkin also featured circuit vaudeville acts - 5 Acts 5 - along with a double bill of movies, silents or later talkies, newsreels, short subjects and kiddie matinee extras (more about that in another chapter).

Henrietta became a fixture with her newly installed Robert Morton pipe organ from the silent days through the late Fifties. Between shows, she and her organ would miraculously rise out of the earth at the left wing of the stage, in a flood of light and color. She would play a few numbers and also accompany the occasional "follow the bouncing ball" sing-along numbers.

I have read several books about Brownsville and searched my rich memory banks and I believe that the glue that held it all together was its people - many were simple and hard-working, but we also had our share of marginal characters, who made it a place of endless fascination.

I wish I could bottle whatever it was we had going in Brownsville. Call it tolerance. Call it acceptance of diversity. It worked. It worked for the Jews and non-Jews alike.

The factors most Brownsvillians had in common were two - they were poor and they were Jews. Most everyone knew or spoke a kind of Yiddish as well as Jewish-American English with a distinct Brooklyn accent. Some lived in crowded airless tenements with broken down stoops, others in dilapidated two-family houses, a few in more affluent apartment buildings. One of my classmates lived in an apartment building on Bristol Street that had an elevator - her father was an assistant district attorney and they even had a maid.

Most everyone was struggling just to get by. Many were immigrants, a sizeable number were first generation American and a smaller group, the children of native-born Americans. The fathers were garment district workers, house painters, plumbers, small merchants. The housewives struggled to put food on the table and clothes on the backs of their families. Some also held down jobs in factories and stores as well.

Jewish denominations as we know them today, were not clearly defined in Brownsville. As we understood it, a shul (synagogue) was a shul. And they were everywhere, often several on one block. By today's strict divisions, they would be considered Orthodox, since the women's area was distinctly separate from the men. This separation (mechitsa) was universally accepted as part of the fabric of life. On the Sabbath morning and at sundown, there were always men coming to and from the various shuls with their embroidered velvet bags containing religious necessities - that was how the street knew what day of the week it was.

Participation in the observance of Shabbes varied. For some it meant mama's candle lighting ritual in the tiny crowded kitchen, followed by a Shabbes dinner. Even those who did not enjoy a full belly during the week, somehow scraped up enough for the festive Shabbes dinner, on their own or through the many Jewish charities that abounded. It would traditionally include a fresh challah, gefilte fish, sweet Concord wine, a golden noodle soup, some kind of roast, a fruit compote made of stewed dried fruits like prunes, apricots, raisins and apples. You drank it down with soda or seltzer, since kosher laws meant you could not have milk with your meal. There might be a kishke (stuffed derma) or heldzl (stuffed chicken neck) or other delicacies from the old country. You might also have baked goods with tea at the end. Our mother always baked wonderful things for Shabbes and holidays. Ice cream was out, because you didn't serve a dairy dessert with a meat meal.

Very strict Orthodox people would have separate dishes and cookware for meat and dairy. We did not, so technically they could not eat in homes like ours, while we could in theirs. But these distinctions were often blurred. It seems to me that today's frum Jews put more emphasis on such matters than they once did. We have a supermarket here in Baltimore that routinely offers special deals for people who are willing to have their kitchens kashered, made ritually kosher. I don't recall one such grocery or butcher shop in all of Brownsville doing the same. It would have been unthinkable.

For the more frum or religious among us, being observant meant the complete cessation of using modern conveniences after sundown Friday or on the eve of a Jewish holiday - no turning on of lights or stoves or radios or record players or other electric appliances. The closest you came to a hot meal, was served from a pot that sat atop the pilot light of the gas stove, low enough to keep the food tepid, but not hot enough to burn it. At the other end of the spectrum, for many others, the Sabbath day, Friday sundown to Saturday sundown, slipped by unnoticed, and its many customs and no-no's not observed by word or ritual.

While keeping kosher kitchens was more or less the norm, only a few of the restaurants bothered to follow religious strictures. So if you chose to eat out on a Shabbes, or even buy a soda, it was in a non-kosher establishment. No one raised an eyebrow.

The stores, except those owned by strict Sabbath observers, the shomer shabbes, not only remained open for business, but the overwhelming majority of their customers were Jews and they were mostly staffed by Jews. Jewish kids flocked to the Saturday movie matinees - the Pitkin, the Palace, the Stadium, the Sutter, the Ambassador, the Tiffany, where their American acculturation continued full-tilt. Public transportation was used without let-up. Jewish housewives in their festive best, primped up baby carriages and strollers in tow, did not hesitate to promenade up and down Pitkin Avenue either to buy things if they could afford them, or do window-shopping if they could not.

For those who went by bus and subway to work in the garment district in Manhattan, only the super-frum would not work on Shabbes or Jewish holidays. My father was one of those who would never turn away work - after all, between lack of work during slack seasons which could add up to 12, 15 weeks a year, and five children to feed and clothe, 7 in all, it would have been irresponsible of him not to work when there was work. And that included the occasional side jobs he got as an alterations tailor for a shop on Strauss Street or as a dresser at the nearby Yiddish theater. This was a prevailing work ethic, one quickly picked up by the new generation, even for those who were still in school and had part-time jobs.

There were unwritten rules for behavior in front of a shul, and these were universally observed even by the most secular. If kids were running or playing on Sabbaths and holidays, they slowed to a walk until they had passed by. If they decided to enter the shul, they did not brandish money - girls left their "pocketbooks" at home, boys put on a yarmulke or other head covering. It was the fashion for young boys to wear scaled down fedoras, called man hats, if they were dressing up for Shabbes or the Jewish holidays, as well as suit and tie. By the same token, I cannot recall a single incident of protest by the frum at modes of dress, going out shopping or to the movies, or protesting the cars going by.

If you entered a shomer Shabbes (Sabbath observer) home, you kissed the mezuzza hanging on the doorpost. If the lights were off, you did not flick them on. You did not expect to play records there or listen to the radio. If there was a piano in the apartment, you would find it closed and you did not open it up, even if you enjoyed such a liberty on a normal weekday. Yet if a frum friend visited you at these times, they did not feel it was their place to lecture you on your degree of observance or non-observance. If a friend was religious, he or she did not give offence and criticize you in your apartment, when you turned the lights on or off, heated up the kettle for tea, played the radio.

There were many kinds of shuls in Brownsville, from storefront affairs to full-scale choir shuls like the Strauss Street shul, where my brother first sang in the choir and then became a soloist. A certain Mr. Wolf, an entrepreneur/agent was struck by his clear, bright boy soprano voice and for a few years, my little brother enraptured worshippers at several synagogues in Brooklyn - until his voice began to change. He sang mostly during the Jewish High Holy Days.

Now the Jewish holiday calendar had an unwritten sliding scale of importance as far as the Jews of Brownsville were concerned. Most of the key holidays saw school closings, or at least special release for Jewish children and teachers. But only on the Passover and Fall line-up of high-powered Holy Days, the Days of Awe, were all the Jewish stores closed. Most of the businesses were closed. A few restaurants remained open. The movies were open. You were all dressed up. Relatives came and went. You went and came back from seeing relatives. Kids walked up and down the streets, from Pitkin Avenue all the way up to Prospect Park and Grand Army Plaza in their finery. Running into the shuls and sitting in for some of the services, was part of the entertainment.

Kids were tolerated until they began to get out of hand. Then they would be sent back out on the street to fend for themselves. There were no special programs for children as there are today.

Upstairs in the women's shul, there was a lot of weeping and wailing. Downstairs, in the men's shul, there was a total lack of order. Everyone davened (prayed) at his or her own speed, and the hum of voices was non-stop. Those davening on the bimah (the altar where the Torah is read) were in tune with themselves. Today everyone is on the same page and well organized.

But the shul across the street from us had a third basement level shul, frequented by old men in black only, men with long payes (ear curls) and long beards. They spoke no English and brooked no noise in their shul. Except for one holiday - Simchas Torah.

And that was sheer magic. First of all, Simchas Torah is a fabulous Jewish holiday, celebrating the end of a year's cycle of Torah reading and the seamless beginning of another. And it is celebrated with dancing around with the Torah scrolls, eating honey cake and drinking wine or whiskey. And for the children, it meant running amok with Simchas Torah paper flags. It could be late September, but mostly it was October.

As the sun would go down, our mothers would secure a raw potato or apple to the top point of the flag stick, make a hole in it and insert a candle in the hole. These candles would be lit after sundown and as the skies grew darker, we would walk or run around in our holiday finery with our lit flag candles. The streets would be semi-deserted as businesses were mostly closed. Lights in the apartment windows would come on and the sky would turn an inky blue-black set off with twinkling stars.

And downstairs in that third shul with the old men in beards, they would be passing out honey cake, bags of peanuts and raisins, rock candy and little paper cups of schnapps. And they made no discrimination as to whom they gave the goodies - little boys, big boys, my 4-year old brother in his man hat. Girls too. You could come back for seconds or thirds. It didn't take very long for kids to feel a little bit merry.

How I loved Simchas Torah in Brownsville. In these so-called kid-centered times, when I berate elders of a 21st century shul as to why they don't have candles in the paper flags, I get the expected answer about safety concerns. Yet, when I think back to those children that we were, well-oiled by the free schnapps, running up and down the shul steps, up to the women's shul, down to the men's shul, outside and down again to the third shul below, in spaces far more cramped and crowded than in any modern day house of worship, it comes to me, that there was never a fire or an accident resulting from this lovely practice.

And nobody ever asked us if our parents were members of the congregation. The only time seats were reserved was during the High Holy Days in those buildings that featured a famous cantor and choir, such as the one my brother sang in.

Jewishness was in our blood and bones and souls. Whether we were religious or secular, American-born, whether our parents came from Poland, Russia, Romania, Hungary, Lithuania or South of the Border, we accepted each other as fellow Jews. There was a term used - MOT, Member of the Tribe.

Weddings and funerals were neighborhood affairs. The comings and goings of the wedding party to the catering establishment always brought out the crowds, even those who didn't know bride and groom personally. Funeral corteges stopped traffic in the streets. And everyone in the neighborhood of Brownsville, from diehard Communist to bearded Orthodox grieved on the day of the funeral of Julius and Ethel Rosenberg, which took place in Brownsville.

Depending on when the counts were taken, the population of Brownsville was anywhere from 80% to 90%. The balance included Blacks, Italians, and a smattering of Irish, Germans, Poles and Russians. While there was some friction between these groups, as a day to day rule, outbreaks of interracial violence, vandalism and offensive graffiti were not the norm.

Of course it is a well-known fact that there were street gangs in Brownsville, as chronicled in "The Amboy Dukes". It is also well-known that Murder, Inc. met for its nefarious purposes at a candy store, Midnight Rose's, downstairs from the elevated IRT subway station at Livonia and Saratoga, across from the Ambassador movie theater. For most of us it was a place to get candy, soda, ice cream and the papers - they didn't bother us, we didn't bother them. Such activities stayed in their own tracks and the average citizen was untouched. Bottom line, you walked the streets of Brownsville without fear. Doors could be left unlocked, even at night. In warm weather, people could sleep on their fire escapes or sun themselves on tar beach (the name for those rickety tarred rooftops) in absolute safety.

I can't think of a neighborhood like that in this day and age.

Mass demonstration for Roosevelt, Henry Wallace and popular Jewish-American Goveror of New York State, Herbert H. Lehman

One picture is worth a thousand words. This pairing of Labor and Roosevelt was a given in places like Brownsville.

One bright sunny afternoon in the autumn of 1944, at the height of his campaign for an unprecedented fourth presidential term, an ailing but smiling Franklin Delano Roosevelt waved from his open-air limo, as it majestically glided along Pitkin Avenue in the heart of Brownsville.

The normally heavy shopping crowds were more than doubled, as the Brownsvillians who normally watched the passing scene peering from their windows or seated on milk boxes and chairs in front of their tenements, added to the melee. Now there were people leaning down over the roofs and teenagers piled on top of other people's cars on the side streets. The entrance areas to the many stores were also packed. Pitkin Avenue parking had been eliminated for the presidential parade, which meant more room for people.

And all of Pitkin Avenue was decked out in banners, cascades and flags of red, white and blue.

Police had roped off the sidewalks to keep the crowds from blocking the roadway itself. Busses and ambulances had been re-routed. Babies and toddlers were either in carriages or perched on parents' shoulders.

The parade was headed in the direction of Eastern Parkway, toward the Loew's Pitkin and Zion Memorial Park where local Democrats would be giving speeches. First you heard drums and brass from a distance, then came the paraders, which included a contingent of Jewish war veterans in full regalia.

It was a stirring sight and yet, in hindsight, kind of curious. Here was one of the poorest neighborhoods in America, in the final bloody year of World War II. Every street had its own roster of Gold Star mothers, grieving for lost sons. Inflation was at fever pitch and shortages and rationing limited options for those who did have work. And then there was the unspoken worry about the survival of relatives in Europe, about whose fate so little was known, so much was feared.

Yet, despite the fact that the war had done little to alleviate economic conditions, to these people, Franklin Delano Roosevelt was a demi-god, a hero, a movie star. His wife Eleanor was much admired as well.

Brownsville had come to applaud, to cheer, almost to worship. Many a tenement kitchen or parlor had his picture on their walls. Sometimes it was beautifully framed. Sometimes it was torn from the Sunday News or Mirror and just pasted.

After all, Roosevelt was now the most powerful leader of the Free World, the greatest icon of the war again Hitler, the quintessential evil-doer of the age, so it was natural he should be adored. But why would this ailing campaigner, with his declining health, take the time to ride down such a downtrodden neighborhood?

Eleanor Roosevelt was a role model for women of such proportion, no woman in or out of politics to date has eclipsed her.

The Liberal Party and the Garment workers Union (ILGWU) forged a powerful alliance that could make or break New York and even national elections. I recognize union leader David Dubinsky (with cigar) and beside him, Mayor Robert L. Wagner.

To understand this, one must have a sense of what Brownsville was all about politically. It was not a two-party town.

Brownsville and politics were inseparable at every level. Every party was represented in the Brownsville political spectrum, Democrats of course, and a smattering of Republicans.

The American Labor Party, a leftist-leaning regional, became identified as a Communist fellow-traveler, so some of its membership drifted into the more centrist Liberal Party. The Liberal Party functioned as a kind of king-maker, ultimately doling out its support to the Democrats, but withholding support to push for progressive planks to the Democratic Party platform.

Voter education, directed at Yiddish-speaking immigrants

Brownsville also housed the Socialist Party, which had been fielding Norman Thomas as a candidate for years and many a socialist-minded voter had to make the agonizing decision to vote his heart and thereby make it easier for the Republican candidate to capture New York's bounty of electoral votes. Or go for the Democratic or Liberal candidate at the crucial moment.

The Socialists also had their problems, as there were various offshoots, such as the Socialist Labor Party, the Socialist Libertarian Party and other splinter groups.

Communists also had had some strength in Brownsville, but when Stalin signed his pact with Hitler, the Communists lost favor with many of their Jewish followers, or at best, left them in a permanent quandary. Their recruiting efforts in Brownsville had focused largely around tenant problems and abuse by landlords - the main technique was promoting so-called Rent Clinics - at which tenants in trouble would come and air their woes, only to be recruited to their cause with brochures and slogans. It must be noted that landlords were bound by rent control, so most tenant complaints centered around maintenance, house painting, plumbing, heating, repairs, utilities and the like.

Margaret Sanger had opened her first family planning clinic on Amboy Street, corner Pitkin and was overwhelmed by local Brownsville housewives even before the doors opened.

Margaret Sanger pictured in front of her short-lived but historic clinic that taught birth control to eager housewives.

Many Brownsville dwellings were far below even sub-standard and plans to build decent housing kept getting bogged down. So there were continuous waves of politicians, local, regional and national, shaking hands at photo ops with activists, industrialists, and local personalities to try to do something to solve Brownsville's terrible housing problem. Everyone talked, but no one got anything done until the Sixties when some of the worst areas were razed and the long-awaited projects were built.

Most of Brownsville's families were fed by the garment industries and every working morning, the men would catch the Pitkin Avenue bus or the subways and travel to Manhattan's garment district. Evenings would see the busses and trains disgorging their weary commuters who had spent the trip home reading the news or discussing politics.

The garment industry is seasonal and there are built-in periods of unemployment called slack seasons - even in the best of times. During those periods the shops that made the garments would simply shut down until the first of the new season samples were ready to be cut. Then there would be a gradual build-up of work, until it peaked with periods of overtime and weekend work. There were two major slack seasons a year.

As a result of Roosevelt's New Deal, there was now unemployment insurance, so that there was at least some money coming into a household during slack season. The power of the unions was strengthened and this benefited the wage negotiating process. Before the season began, making every garment was broken down into steps, and a price was negotiated for each step. Each completed task was paid for by tickets which the shop steward collected and these were turned into much-needed pay packets. The busy season also meant overtime and on rare occasions, time and a half and double time. Naturally, management tried to pay as little as possible and sometimes negotiations would break down, and strikes would follow.

Most of Brownsville's working force were either members of a trade union such as the ILGWU (International Ladies Garment Workers Union) or at least union-friendly. Or they were in the union-based home improving trades - painters, plumbers and the like. Mr. Spivack, who lived third floor front in our building was both a boss painter, always clad in paint-spattered white pants and painter's hat, but also an ardent and vocal Communist, who had a hard time defending Stalin after his pact with Hitler, especially as the word filtered out as to the tragic events in Europe.

At the simplest level, the two domestic enemies of Brownsville were the Landlords and the Bosses. The litmus test for a politician was whether he was for the working people, or in the pay of the Bosses and the Landlords. And Roosevelt scored very high as an enemy of the Bosses and the Landlords.

Politics was everywhere in Brownsville. Everyone read at least two publications called "papers" daily, one in English if they could. Popular Brownsville papers included the News and Mirror, the then highly-liberal New York Post, the Daily Worker (Communist) and Socialist Worker (Trotskyist). Yiddish readers got their take on the news from the social-democrat, pro-union Forverts (The Forward), the slightly more conservative Der Tog (The Day), the religious Morgn Zhurnal (Morning Journal) and the Communist "Freiheit" (Freedom). Union and organizational publications, with their influential columns and editorials, came in the mail and were just as avidly read.

In addition, at the colorful newsstands located along Pitkin Avenue, or next to subway stops, you could find a variety of monthly publications, also highly political in nature, in English, Yiddish and German.

Political headquarters, were housed either in prime locations on avenue-facing second floor lofts, or vacant store fronts. These places held flyers and brochures, bulky banners and signs and served as meeting spaces. In between they were informal spaces for socializing and discussing the hot issues of the moment. And every one of the headquarters had a mimeo machine to create instant handouts, plus an addressograph with names and addresses of people that could be targets of mailings. Most of the people who toiled in these places were volunteers, true believers.

Every campaign or local crisis occasioned a street meeting. The party would procure a permit, rent or trot out a street corner platform, rustle up some volunteers and create an event. Sometimes their main speaker was a celebrity and that would mean some police in the area for crowd control. These events would be promoted by passing out flyers. The corner of Herzl and Pitkin and the corner of Hopkinson and Pitkin were among the favorites. Every party used this method to reach out to the people. Volunteers walked about with slogan-bearing signs and handouts that highlighted their talking points, along with a pitch for money and volunteers and urgings to write your congressman or senator.

Now the people who gathered at these meetings were fairly opinionated, so they would feel free to break in and shout their dissenting remarks. Sometimes it was the odd man in the street who would heckle. Other times it would be an organized affair - the Communists traditionally came out to heckle the Socialists and they came prepared to argue their party platform chapter and verse.

For his part, Roosevelt was aware of how important a neighborhood such as Brownsville could be. In the past campaign, the density of Brownsville's voting population may have supplied the winning margin he needed to carry New York State, and therefore was terribly important again in 1944.

There may also have been a little back history at play. When Roosevelt ran for Governor against Republican Ottinger, a Jew, in fact, the first Jewish Gubernatorial candidate in New York State, he barely scraped a victory of 25,000, less than 1 percent of 4,000,000 ballots cast. Brownsville, the most heavily Jewish district in the state, produced for the Roosevelt-Lehman ticket its greatest majority ever for a Democrat - against the first Jewish candidate for Governor. The Democratic leader of Brownsville was Hymie Shorenstein, the only non-Irish leader of a political district in all of Brooklyn at that time.

Harry Truman also made such a visit in 1948, but it was kind of anti-climactic. He had never achieved the iconic level of Roosevelt - and Brownsville had lost its innocence in the later revelations about Roosevelt's policies vis a vis rescuing Europe's Jews.

Paper sellers brought the news in Yiddish to readers of all political and religious persuasions. Makeshift rolling stores were set up on old baby carriages like these. My mother had one such arrangement for a shopping cart.

Community activism was contagious. This community clean-up demonstration took place at Amboy Street corner Pitkin - the garbage cans say 38 Amboy, a street memorialized in the gang story, "The Amboy Dukes". It was also the street on which, earlier, Margaret Sanger had started her first clinic.

*Rosie the Riveter, was the iconic woman working in a factory,
doing men's tough jobs like welding and riveting, to free a man for
the service. Another version of her, Swingshift Maisie,
was immortalized in a series of popular films by Ann Southern.*

The reality of America's entry into World War II on Sunday, December 7th, 1941 did not hit home for me until the next day at school. My parents had spoken of it in hushed voices to each other that evening - but not to us. However, the next day in school, at P.S. 175, we heard of and spoke of nothing else. I could already imagine the roar of Japanese and German bombers flying over the streets of Brownsville - on certain nights, I could even see lights in the sky, the gleam of bombs headed for Pitkin Avenue --and this palpable fear lasted for me until V-E Day in 1945.

Brownsville went to war with body, mind, heart and soul and a distinct Yiddish accent. The vast political spectrum of Brownsville was suddenly unified - from fiery Communists like Mr. Spivack, the Boss Painter, to the most Orthodox among us. You saw the war, felt it, tasted it - it was everywhere.

On Sabbaths and holidays, it became a common sight to see our local service-men on leave, hanging around the shuls, with their prayer shawls (originally received as Bar Mitzvah presents) now wrapped around their U.S. Army uniforms.

The red, white and blue was everywhere in the form of flags draped from front-facing tenement windows, as banners in store windows and over store entrances. Patriotic posters were everywhere for bond drives and propaganda messages to inform or keep up civilian morale.

Parades were a common event and you never knew when they would pop up - suddenly on any given weekday you would hear faint music in the distance, usually from the direction of East New York, heading towards the Zion Memorial Park, a small triangle of a park facing the Loew's Pitkin. Inevitably, Jewish War Veterans of WWI, including the Women's Auxiliary in white soldier hats and gold lettered bandoliers, would be in the lead. Then there would be appropriate flag raisings and lowerings, taps for the lost soldiers and of course speeches and speeches. There would be parades for the holidays, for candidates, for blood drives. Sometimes schools would participate in full band uniform. Sometimes a movie celebrity would show up in an open car, complete with cortege. It was very colorful. After a while, parades became almost normal and people paid little attention to them and even the strollers and shoppers went about their business as soon as the streets were free to cross.

Sculptural details on the little stage of Zion Memorial Park, which was the focus and end point of many parades and demonstrations. See appendix for details of the park's history.

My kid sister tells me she could squeeze through those bars.
But one day she got stuck.

Many a street-facing window bore witness to a more serious kind of involvement - a small banner with one or more blue stars, indicating that this family had sons in the service. It was a badge of honor - but it was also an indication of worry and concern, almost a prayer, for their safety. Streets often organized into associations and these associations also put up special Roll of Honor boards listing the names of "our boys in the service" with red stars for the living, and a special section of gold stars for those killed in battle.

Can't tell if the flag in the first floor window is a blue or gold star.
These window reminders were everywhere.

Gold star banners hung in mute sadness in some windows, and so-called Gold Star Mothers were treated with compassion and respect. They often marched in the parades on Pitkin Avenue.

One such Gold Star mother, Mrs. Gordon, lived in our building on Herzl corner Pitkin, And we knew the family quite well. The daughter, Lillian, had been my babysitter when I was a baby. And I had been in and out of their apartment many times - happiest when allowed to have a candy from the blue glass music box shaped like a grand piano - they were always the same candies, a chewy hard outer surface with fruity innards when you bit through. Lillian's brother, Eli, played the jazz saxophone, sometimes professionally and I had heard enough jazz in the movies to know he was good. Their windows faced onto the same inner courtyard as my brothers' room and the courtyard would fill up with the sound of his wail when he practiced on a summer afternoon.

My parents slept in the so-called living room with pullout convertible, my sister and I shared a bed in the girls' room and my three brothers slept in bunk beds, two and one, in a tiny room with just enough space for the built-in closet door and room door to swing open and shut. The room also held a maple chest of drawers and a desk. I liked that spot summertimes, because the courtyard with its 15 foot drop below street level was cool, and you could see some of what was going on in the other apartments - a forerunner to "Rear Window"?

Eli Gordon was killed on Anzio Beach - his named appeared on the Roll of Honor.

But even today, I can hear his wailing saxophone, as I remember looking out into the cool courtyard from my brothers' tiny bedroom.

The American-Jewish community in general, and Brownsville was no exception, took deep pride in its own heroes. Two of the well-known poster boys were Sergeant Meyer Levin, a decorated Air Force Hero, and the world-famous Mickey Marcus, who was later to play a key role in the development of newly-born Israel's defense forces. Master Sergeant Levin was a decorated B-17 bombardier in the Pacific theater. His picture appeared in the Yiddish papers, after he survived a flight that claimed the life of Captain Colin Kelly. And also in January, 1943, when his plane ran out of fuel and the crew had to parachute to safety.

Sgt. Levin remained on board long enough to drop a life raft and rescue the crew. This heroic gesture cost him his life.

Mickey Marcus started out in Brownsville, but the family moved up to the more upscale Midwood. After a heroic career in WWII, he moved up to a key role in Israel's war of independence, during which he tragically lost his life. His exploits are chronicled in a film with Kirk Douglas, "Cast A Big Shadow."

The fear of enemy attack at home set in motion a program of blackouts and brownouts, designed to keep the outlines of the city dark to enemy flyers from above. You could not put on lights at night without pulling down a special window shade. Car bumpers had to be painted half black. And every building had an air raid warden. Mr. Becker was ours. During air raid drills, when the sirens went off, he would check for escaping window lights and ring the bell to let anyone know who was in violation. Air raid wardens also patrolled the streets and made people put out cigarettes, cigars and pipes that might give aid to the enemy.

In the schools we had both fire drills and air raid drills. In a fire drill, you lined up in your classroom and marched out of the school in orderly fashion. It was always pleasant to break up the day and see the outside world. Air raid drills meant everyone went quickly to the corridors and sat, class by class, on the floor, and we sang songs like "Deep in the Heart of Texas" until the All Clear sounded.

Brownsville school kids were deeply involved in the war effort. In Betsy Head Park, the park across from P.S. 175, for instance, under the guidance of Miss Cherichetti, the Assistant Principal, the kids planted and harvested a Victory Garden - tending it was partly done during school time and some of it after school on a volunteer basis.

Kids collected grease cans which were needed for glycerine in the manufacture of bombs. They collected used tires for the rubber. Brownsville kids helped with everything from blood drives to raising funds for starving war orphans overseas. Some were school or class-run activities. Others were done on individual initiative and the collections were duly turned over to the appropriate authorities.

War bond drives were a nationwide effort and Brownsville raised a huge sum of money for a working class neighborhood - 15 million dollars. Kids participated through Savings Stamps books, which, when you filled one up to the lordly sum of $18.75, could be converted into a single $25 War Bond. It was a heady thought that this same $18.75 was not only helping us defeat Hitler and Tojo and Mussolini - BUT that in ten years each of these bonds would be worth $25 apiece. Keep in mind that $18 represented a normal month's rent in our neighborhood.

War Bonds were promoted in the movie theaters, especially the Loew's Pitkin, in parades, on the radio, with posters, through the schools. They became a patriotic gift for weddings, Bar Mitzvahs, Sweet Sixteens, even as gifts for newborns. Many workers gave a portion of their much-needed pay packets towards purchase of War Bonds.

As the war dragged on, all kinds of regulating measures came into effect. Rent, wage and price controls helped fence in inflation which was spiraling rapidly - inflation was a common topic of conversation on summer evenings, as neighbors sat on chairs and milk crates in front of their doorsteps. And then there was rationing.

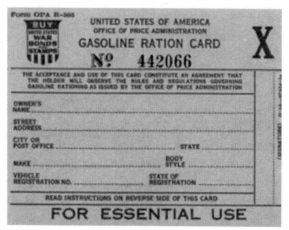

Gasoline ration card X. Unrestricted access to gasoline. There were 698,352 issued between May 15-June 30, 1942.

Rationing meant the controlled availability of foodstuffs and other goods in short supply and/or needed for the war effort. It involved meat, sugar, coffee, nylons, gasoline, canned goods and so much more. Different items were worth different points. And every family was issued a different amount of spendable points each month. When you purchased these items at the store, you not only paid for it with money, but you also had to surrender the appropriate number of coupons for that item. If you ran out of coupons, even if you had double the money, you could not buy the item except through the flourishing and illegal black market. The amount of coupons issued to a family depended on size and sometimes, special considerations. The only time I encountered the back market was on the movie screen - where they were equal to gangsters and Nazi spies.

Rationing meant it was not enough to have money to buy needed foods and other goods - you had to have the points as well. Books were issued according to the size and needs of a family. And you had to pay with both money and coupons. Except for the black market (which was illegal) if you used up your coupons, you couldn't buy the item even for double the price. Out of points, out of luck.

Housewives were always on the lookout for ways and recipes to conserve their coupon supply. My mother had come upon a recipe for meatless chopped liver. Chopped liver was a favorite dish in our house, especially for sandwiches. It was made with pan-fried string beans and onions and chopped fine. The color was a little greenish, but it satisfied somewhat. I have since tried without success to recreate this recipe.

One way to cut down on meat consumption was the nationwide observance of Meatless Tuesday. You could not buy meat that day and were urged to eat non-meat dishes. Consequently Hymie the Butcher would be closed on Tuesdays, as would Shapiro's Kosher Delicatessen, whose main offerings were pickled tongue, pastrami, hot dogs and specials (extra plump sausages) and such. For Jews it was easy - we just went dairy and we had a rich heritage of recipes in that category. My mother used to make a vegetable soup for lunch, swimming in milk and butter. But it was always odd, on a Tuesday afternoon, with all the other shops in high gear, to see the shuttered down butcher shops and delis.

"Send a salami to your boy in the Army" was a slogan started by Katz's delicatessen on the Lower East Side. Yes, food parcels were a big part of wartime collection efforts. Sending kosher food and ethnic delicacies to our soldier boys in the States and on the battlefronts, was a high priority for Brownsville households.

But people of Brownsville were also mindful of European relations lost in the mists of war and consequently there were drives for bundles of food and clothing for Russia. Landsmanschafften, organizations of immigrants from specific towns and shtetls, were very active here. Funds were constantly being raised for the Joint Jewish Distribution Committee, and for Hias, a Jewish organization helping refugees to get to what was then known as Palestine. Every household had a pushka, collection box, for these purposes.

Politics and propaganda (call it morale-building) were everywhere and on every tongue, in every language. You were informed about the war through the newspapers, radio and the movie houses. Political parties took every opportunity to erect a platform and make speeches, especially evenings after dinner time. Occasionally there were block parties in conjunction with bond drives, and these were a treat, because there were live bands and dancing and sometimes celebrity guests.

Some married men were called to arms as well - Jack Hart became a soldier in the latter part of the war, but was not sent overseas. Our father was not called, because he had five children and was overage as well, so we were spared. But for those whose sons and fathers were in uniform, there was knitting of khaki colored socks and sweaters, and of course, the star on the window.

The films themselves were the most effective propaganda for the war effort. Action films demonized the enemy as audiences booed, and deified the war heroes as audiences cheered. One pattern that emerged was the much-needed comedy relief character - usually from Brooklyn, and more or less Jewish. "Da Brooklyns" were played by stars like John Garfield and a host of familiar character players of the period. For us, they were the hometown heroes. More subtle films showed the struggles of brave wives and families coping with the absence of loved ones. Others dealt with brave deeds of underground and resistance fighters. There were spy movies and mystery movies, and even Sherlock Holmes found himself caught in a time warp, reappearing in 1943 to catch Nazi spies.

One of Brownsville's favorite sons made a tremendous contribution to wartime morale - namely, David Daniel Kaminsky, born in Brownsville on January 18, 1913. The 3rd son of an immigrant tailor from the Ukraine, and the only one born in the United States, he was destined for a stellar career in show business as Danny Kaye. A dropout of Thomas Jefferson High in adjacent East New York, he eventually came to Hollywood, where his wartime films helped take the sting out of all our wartime troubles.

There was always time for graffiti humor, and most of it was in the form of mocking Hitler, Tojo or Hirohito and of course, Mussolini. But the single most prevalent piece of graffiti was of course, the ubiquitous "Kilroy was Here" which was even, according to legend, found in Hitler's most secret installations, filling him with fear about the efficiency of America's spying capabilities.

The saddest time of the war in Brownsville occurred on April 12, 1945, with victory in sight. I was playing, just after supper, in front of Jack Diamond's men's haberdashery. Someone came by and asked us kids if we had heard that Roosevelt had died at Warm Springs, Georgia. It was as if the very air had been taken away from us. We had known no other president in our short lifetimes.

The most joyous time for me was V-E Day. We had defeated Hitler and his evil minions and the killing would stop. We had not yet, in this first euphoria, learned the true extent of the Nazi horrors, the Holocaust, the slaughter of our relatives, six million of our people. But it was Victory. And life as we knew it came to a joyous, tearful halt. Strangers embraced strangers. Trucks with blaring sound systems came through the streets. Preparations were rapidly begun for block parties throughout Brownsville. Kids ran up and down streets, stairs and hallways, shouting, "THE WAR IS OVER! Cars tooted their horns, and people didn't know whether to laugh or cry. Kids were climbing into trucks and getting free rides around the neighborhood.

My brother Elliott asked my mother if the war was over. "Yes", she said. "It's over."

I personally did not experience the final end of the war, V-J Day, in Brownsville, since I was away at Camp. So I missed out on the revelries. For me, away at camp, it was a more muted experience of songs and speeches in the camp dining room that evening.

And when I returned to Brownsville, it was to a changed place, with new problems and a new focus.

Shortly after the war ended, my mother was walking down our street, when she heard someone call out her name, the name she was known by in the Old Country. Emma. Emma Basson. Running to her from across the street was a tall woman with reddish brown hair topped with a crown of braids. Her name was Sarah Medansky and she was a distant relation, a Holocaust survivor from her home town of Vilna in what is now Lithuania. They embraced and laughed and cried together. What a sight it must have been - our plump little mama, no bigger than 4 foot 7, hugging this gaunt woman of about 5'8". And what tragic news Sarah Medansky carried with her.

Over a cup of coffee in our tiny kitchen, Sarah Medansky brought sad closure to years or worry and fear over the survival of her large family - father, stepmother, brothers, a sister (two others had long emigrated to Canada and South Africa), their spouses and children, and an army of cousins and friends. They family had all been rousted out of my grandfather's apartment and slaughtered. Why had she survived when all the rest had perished? She told us that she had worked in the German army kitchens and was not in the ghetto when the roundup occurred.

Afterwards, when Sarah returned from work to the ruins of the Vilna ghetto, she looked in on our grandfather's apartment and found all the furniture overturned - they had struggled and not gone to their deaths like sheep. She also said it was Poles and Lithuanians who did the rounding up, not Nazi soldiers.

Somehow she made it through, and in the wartime aftermath, landed in the DP camps in Germany. There she married a nice quiet man and they produced a little daughter, Chanele, on whom they lavished unusual love and care. And in a unique twist of fate, Sarah Medansky, found herself living on the same street as our mother.

I later learned from the sole-surviving nephew that they had been shot at Ponar, a former military fort and later a place for picnicking that had been turned into a site for mass shootings and burials of Vilna's Jews. I later learned this last roundup, the final one, took place on September 23, 1943 and my family perished along with thousands of other Jews from the Vilna ghetto. Vilna, the Jerusalem of Europe, site of learnng and Jewish culture, reduced to nothing. Its Jews, shot, starved, or murdered in the ghetto and death camps. I try to remember to light a memorial candle on September 23 every year.

It's important to know that to us in Brownsville, the disclosures about the 6,000,000 who perished, the camps, the ovens and the tragic remains were very personal, not just the statistics and horror stories we saw in our newsreels and newspapers. Many of the surviving remnant found their way to the DP camps of Germany, and the Hias, Joint and other organizations issued daily lists of these people as they passed through their gates. My father became totally immersed, even obsessed, in scanning these lists, mainly in the Yiddish Forward, for family, townspeople, anyone he or my mother might have known. A remnant of about 250,000 Jews found themselves in these UNNRA camps, their movement stalled by quotas and red tape in potential host countries such as the US and Canada.

Father found a few unrelated survivors from his home shtetl of Malat, north of Vilna, to whom he reached out, and one day, came upon the name of my mother's nephew, Eliezer Basson. He had escaped, along with a brother, and had served in the Russian army. His brother was killed in the fighting, and Eliezer, known in the family as Leizer, had lost an eye. Upon returning to Vilna after the war, he saw the ruins, and understood that this was no longer his home.

One Yiddish song, also sung in English, was very popular in Brownsville. It poignantly expressed the national Jewish feeling of uprootedness.

Vi Ahin Zol Ikh Geyn
Music: S. Korn-Tuer
Lyrics: O. Strock

Der Yid vert geyogt un geplogt	*The Jew is chased and persecuted.*
Nisht zikher iz far im yeder tog	*No day is sure for him.*
Zayn lebn iz a finstere nakht	*His life is a dark night.*
Zayn shtrebn alts far im iz farmakht	*His striving is blocked at every turn.*
Farlozn bloyz mit sonim kayn fraynt	*He is left only with enemies, no friends.*
Kayn hofnung on a zikhern haynt	*No hope without a secure today.*

Refrain

Vi ahin zol ikh geyn?	*Tell me where can I go?*
Ver kon entfern mir?	*Who can answer me?*
Vi ahin zol ikh geyn?	*Where can I go?*
Az farshlosn z'yede tir	*Every door is closed to me.*
S'iz di velt groys genug	*The world is big enough*

Nor far mir iz eng un kleyn	*But for me it's crowded and small.*
Vi a blik kh'muz tsurik I	*If I try to return*
S'iz tsushtert yede brik	*Every bridge is closed.*
Vi ahin zol ikh geyn?	*Tell me where can I go?*

When my father found his name, Leizer was in one of the DP camps. Father alerted the Basson clan in the Bronx , my mother's family, which had an active cousins' circle. They offered to bring him to America and set him up. Leizer refused - there was only one home for him - the Jewish homeland, Eretz Yisroyl, then called Palestine and still under British rule. And to Palestine he went, where after helping the Haganah to rescue Jewish refugee children, he became a shepherd in a kibbutz in the Jordan Valley. He married a survivor from Bulgaria and they built a family together. I always felt the lack of a place, a cemetery, a headstone, something to stand by and physically mourn the loss of my bobe/zeyde, grandmother and grandfather, indeed, the entire European Basson family. Decades later, I was able to visit my surviving cousin Leizer at his kibbutz - and there in a memorial garden, in a kibbutz filled with aging survivors, was a plaque honoring the families that had perished. And there for the first time, the only time, was something concrete to stand in front of and weep. Yes, the Holocaust is a very personal experience.

I have always envied those who got to know and have a relationship with their grandparents. History denied this to me and my siblings. But Tante Brokhe and Uncle Moishe substituted for grandparents in our lives and I shall always be grateful for this.

I became friendly with a refugee of my age named Bronya Zatz. She was the youngest of five and had four brothers, along with very religious parents. They were from Poland, but had escaped to Russia under harrowing circumstances. There they were eventually captured and separated. She got through the war all alone. Little red-haired, pale-skinned Bronya made a vow - that if by some miracle her entire family were to survive and be reunited, she would become super frum, super religious, just like her parents. She wound up, after the war, in a DP camp in Frankfurt and after some effort by the Allied authorities, located them all, safe and sound. And Bronya kept her promise - her faith intact. As did her parents. Her four older brothers however, emerged secular, unbelieving and cynical. Same outcome, different conclusion. They all lived together in a Brownsville apartment. Their home was strictly observant, her mother always wore a wig and a scarf, and her father had a thick gray beard. Many of our best talks happened while we were taking long walks along Pitkin Avenue on a Sabbath or Jewish holiday afternoon.

I also had the pleasure of linking up, in French class, with 3 girls from France, originally from Poland, also DP's. They taught me current French slang and culture, and it went a long way to helping me shine in learning that language, while I helped them in learning about how things worked in Brownsville.

My fluent Yiddish opened many doors to me with the newly arrived refugee survivors, my mother used to call them "di grine", the greenhorns. On the far corner of Herzl Street, at No. 8, there lived a settlement of grine, all from the city of Lodz, which had been a center of the garment industry in Poland and in which many Jews had been involved at every level from sweat shop laborers to owners. These were mostly young men, some single, a few married with Polish nicknames like Anyush. The youngest among them they humorously called Junior - he was now about twenty-one.

They spoke Yiddish and Polish among themselves and they had accepted me easily into their company as we gathered in front of their building some evenings. They spoke about the Lodz ghetto and individuals they knew. And also about their mutual time in the concentration camp of Auschwitz. One of the most chilling things I heard was that when they first entered the camps, it was the fatter people who died first. They concurred among themselves that food deprivation hit the obese the hardest.

The married couple at No. 8 once asked me to babysit their newborn for a special evening out. I remember feeling there was something odd, something missing in the apartment. There were newly bought tchatchkes, gimcrackery, a few prints on the wall, new curtains and appliances, there was a fresh coat of paint of the walls. And they had left me food in the refrigerator to nibble on if I got hungry. There was a wedding photo, taken in the DP camp where they met, in a small frame on a mahogany lamp table - but still something was missing.

And then it hit me. There were no family photos - no pictures of grandparents, relations, childhood pictures. There was no history to clutter up their décor. These people had come from rubble and bones and were starting all over again from nothing. It made me shudder.

But there was a dark side to this new influx of people to Brownsville. As the postwar boom allowed some residents to move to richer neighborhoods, these "grine" moved in. Some of these moves helped remove rent control guards so landlords could raise the rent. Various refugee organizations helped subsidize their housing, found them work, helped furnish their homes.

But what rankled many old-timers was that the very landlord improvements which had eluded them most - new appliances, upgrades in plumbing and heating, painting and plastering - the refugees got it all. There was anger and resentment.

There were a number of dark allegations that emerged - someone like Sarah Medansky survived because she must have consorted with the German soldiers. Those boys who survived Auschwitz, survived because they did dirty things to survive. Maybe they ratted on their fellow prisoners or did sonderkommando tasks, (sorting remains, gold teeth, spectacles) with the crematoria.

These suspicions lurked in the very atmosphere.

On the other hand, these survivors were initially "damaged goods" - they had undergone such traumas as the human mind, body and soul could barely tolerate.

So they did not come hat in hand, overflowing with thanks to their American rescuers and sponsors. They had baggage - personal memories of betrayal by long-trusted neighbors and even fellow Jews. They had been physically and psychologically abused for over five years. And had lost everything, everyone that meant anything to them.

And liberation had been no picnic - they encountered virulent anti-Semitism if they tried to return home. Their first experiences after liberation from their camps and hiding places, shell-shocked and almost dead, had been to be herded into DP camps in of all places, Germany. There, under seemingly interminable detention, barely different from concentration camps, they awaited an uncertain fate.

It's not that America's Jews were unsympathetic to their plight and tragic history - but many felt the refugees believed the world now owed them a living, while they the old-timers, continued to toil under the old conditions and no one was cutting them a break.

This was particularly true in Brownsville, where poor housing had been a long-standing sore issue about which nothing was happening but lip service.

One set of grine that became very important to our family was a young man who, together with his sister, had been separated from their parents in Holland and hidden by Dutch citizens. Orphaned like so many others, Arnie and Theo van der Horst were found and brought to the States by their aunt and uncle. And when Arnie met my sister Lakie almost a decade later, they meshed and became a couple, married and raised two sons. For decades, Arnie spoke little of his wartime experiences and traumas as a hidden child, but recently, he began to speak out in public and is now sharing what happened to him with a whole new generation.

Escorted by American soldiers, a large transport of children survivors of Buchenwald file out of the main gate of the camp, April 27, 1945. They are being taken to homes and medical centers in France. Eli Wiesel appears as the fourth child in the left column.

The film "The Best Years of Our Lives" is a powerful mirror of what life was like for returning war veterans and their families and I watch it religiously every time it pops up on my screen. I smile a little when I realize that most of the younger movie buffs watching it will miss a tiny little detail - the veteran's lapel pin worn by ex-GI's figures significantly in unspoken interactions between some of the characters, major and minor.

I saw the movie of course, at the Loew's Pitkin in 1947, the year it came out and it won seven Academy Awards, two of which went to the unknown, untried Harold Russell, for his performance as Homer Parrish, the returning handicapped sailor. I could least relate to the lavish elevator apartment which welcomed home Frederic March, former banker Al Stephenson and even that of Homer - the spacious Boone City one-family houses and wide well-manicured front lawns.

But the shanty which housed the father and stepmother of Fred Derry, the soda jerk, was a lot more accessible to my experience. Even more so, the apartment of his wife, who had moved closer to her job in a nightclub, rang a familiar chord. As the responsible eldest of five children, I had begun earning money as a babysitter. One of my clients was Stella, who lived with her sister Doris and her little boy David in a tiny apartment in our building. It was furnished in taste similar to that of Fred's wife. I could almost smell the heavy hanging perfume and stale cigarettes, hear the coming and going of different boyfriends. Stella and Doris were thought of as "fast" girls. They had a very scantily furnished kitchen, but the little living room contained great jazz, the very first I ever heard, sexy bestseller novels and ashtrays full of cigarette stubs, which I practiced smoking on.

We had gotten so used to the skimpy short clothing fostered by the war powers to save on fabric, that Dior's 1947 New Look created a sensation with its waspy waists, long flowing skirts and an exhuberent new feminism swept the fashion world by storm and Pitkin Ave. rapidly reclaimed its fashion leadership role, featuring the look in its windows. Still, on our block, it was Stella and Doris who wore it first. The men they dated had an aura of small time gangsterism about them and mostly it was they who paid me my babysitting fees and then some. I know from photos they had taken and souvenir matchbooks that many of these dates were at famous nightclubs and I pictured scenes right out of the noir films that were then so prevalent.

But one night when I went upstairs to babysit David, as they were leaving, Stella told me to be very careful this evening. I was to sit with the lights out, read, but not turn on the radio or phonograph, and not answer if anyone rang the door-bell before they returned home around two or three in the morning. No matter what. About ten o'clock, there was a knock at the door. I froze in fear, but did not move a muscle. A man kept calling out for Stella and then Doris, his lan-guage growing more agitated and insulting. He banged and kicked on the door, which was very thin. Little separated the outside of the door from where I was sitting, cowering. Eventually, thankfully, he grew tired, and stomped downstairs. When the girls returned, I told them what had happened - and they gave me ten dollars. It was a fortune.

Little by little work picked up, as the garment district shifted from military to consumer manufacture, and my father began enjoying shorter slack seasons, more overtime. But it was not instantaneous prosperity. He always told me that the garment industry was the first to feel the pinch of hard times such as the depression, and the last to pick up and get the benefit, when prosperity returned. And this slow shift towards prosperity worked itself through Brownsville, which was so heavily dependent upon the garment trade. In truth, hard times for garment workers lasted even through the Roosevelt pre-war years, except that there was now social security instead of hunger and reliance upon a scatter of Jewish charity organizations. The war had seen an uptick due to mili-tary orders and the fact that people could not spend on much but what they wore on their backs. But it was hardly a boom.

Pent-up consumer demand after the war, brought the arrival of new refrigerators and stoves which had not been available since the war. New model cars began to arrive. And TV became the hot new thing to own, with TV commercials generat-ing demand for the new appliances, especially with so many young couples get-ting married and starting families so quickly.

New TV stores began to appear on Pitkin Avenue, some run by returning veterans.

There were so many returning veterans all over the country that competition for jobs was fierce. And Brownsville was no exception. In some cases, employers were obliged to re-hire former employees, but if they wanted too much money, a way would be found to close out the job and get rid of them anyway.

Inflation ran rampant and the housing shortage was acute. Many chose to go back to school and take advantage of the GI Bill.

Others who could manage it, took advantage of another provision of the GI Bill and they bought homes in other parts of Brooklyn, in Queens and Long Island. And thus began the first stages of the exodus from Brownsville.

For those who could not yet leave, and for whom the lure of marriage and babies was too strong to resist, creative housing solutions had to be found.

The old two-family homes often had basements which had been used as club-rooms for necking and petting parties - now they became starter apartments for young couples. I babysat in several of these - most memorable as a babysitting visit, was a tiny dark 2-1/2 room basement apartment painted in Chinese red with Chinese style furniture crowded in it.

As returning servicemen went back to school on the GI Bill, their wives would have to bear the brunt of earning a living and this opened up new opportunities for women, who would normally have remained home while their husbands worked. Expectations for women had been traditionally limited, both in terms of job and education expectations. Filtered through my own lens it came down to this: you hopefully would graduate from High School, hold down a job as book-keeper, stenographer or some such until marriage. If you were very, very bright, you might go to college for four years and become a teacher. In this period, you would get engaged, ideally right after your Sweet Sixteen, open a joint account and save up enough money for a nice wedding and to start married life. The war changed all that - engagements were delayed and of course dating opportunities limited. And women moved into areas they had not explored before.

There was a longer period of being in charge of one's own earnings, of buying what you wanted and staying single a little longer. Women liked the independ-ence of being wage-earners and here was the beginning of the 2-income family when they did finally marry. The grandparents took care of the children by day, with the help of such institutions as the HES and its many child-centered pro-grams. And by the time the husbands graduated from college and entered the business world, the post-war babies were in school and it was so easy to contin-ue the pattern of both parents being away in the daytime. It was then time to buy a house, move into a coop or at least a more upscale neighborhood.

The first real sign of success was that you could move away from Brownsville.

There was still anti-Semitism in the marketplace, a fact that was common knowledge then in Brownsville, but is now almost forgotten. Being Jewish could work against you in getting certain jobs, particularly with large blue chip companies. One such company was Bell Telephone. Only a tiny quota of Jews were hired by them - even those who scored high on the employment exam would be routinely refused with ad hoc excuses - left-handedness, height, weight. Imagine such excuses in today's world.

We didn't quite move away - but we did finally leave the 3-room apartment on Herzl Street for a 6-room railroad apartment with a porch roof. It was the only apartment in a little building corner of Legion and Dumont and it sat atop a billiard parlor. At last, there was a separate bedroom for our parents, a girls bedroom with a 3/4 size bed for two, and a boys' bedroom with two beds that slept all three of our brothers. The kitchen opened out onto the porch which we used as a patio in the good weather. And there was even an extra room with no windows, which we used as a walk-in pantry. If felt almost luxurious.

We even got a telephone for the first time. And a TV set.

Pitkin Avenue became even more of a shoppers' mecca than ever. Even those who had managed to move on up and out of Brownsville came there to shop and visit relatives still in residence. The fashion stores pulsated from season to season with new looks after new looks - changes in hemlines, shapes, fabrics, colors. The soaped-up summer vacation windows would be eyed with keen interest until after the August 15th "reveal".

New furniture was being cranked out and bought on the installment plan. Appliances stores went absolutely wild, as people could not even begin to sate long pent-up appetites for stoves, refrigerators, new work-saving electric appliances and of course, TV's, which blared via loudspeakers onto the streets.

And yes, people dressed up to go shopping on Pitkin Avenue - men in fedoras and suit and tie, women with hats, high heels and gloves.

Installment buying became far more commonplace than before the war as consumer confidence soared. The seeds of our credit-based economy were sown in this boom era - where previously it was a mentality of "watch the pennies" and "save for a rainy day." If you wanted something before that and you didn't have the money, that was it - or you might save up for it - our mother was big on Christmas Clubs - you deposited a certain sum into a special savings account called a Christmas Club, and once a year, you cashed it in. Another method was the layaway plan, in which the store set aside the desired object for you and when you had paid off its price, the object, be it a coat or a TV set, was yours.

One of our European cousins was famous for greeting young couples in the family with "Hello, children, you saving much?" What's interesting is that by this time, this style of thinking was obsolete.

People's leisure lives were scheduled around TV programs. Those who did not have sets, watched in the living rooms of those who did. Watching prime time TV favorites like Milton Berle on Tuesdays, Show of Shows on Saturday was a party affair with snacks and sodas. Our father was working like never before. The kids were getting part-time after-school jobs and bringing in a little money, as well as gratifying their own whims. My brother Elliot, while at the age when today's kids would be carried to Soccer games in SUV's, worked in a shoe store as a salesman. Another brother, Leibl, started out washing glassware at a medical lab, and then began as a shop assistant in a hardware store on Belmont Avenue.

Birthdays and special events were celebrated with more emphasis on gadgets and luxury items than before. And because of my brother's exposure to the latest gadgetry, our mother was showered with work-saving appliances on Mother's Day, her birthday and other holidays

Not only was Pitkin Avenue booming as a shopping mecca - there was a store on Livonia Avenue, Fortunoff's, that kept expanding. It was a favorite for sourcing wedding gifts like china, silver, glass, tchatchkes. But instead of growing on one premises, the owners moved into more and more stores close by and put their name on them. You could buy linens, antiques, collectibles and the name even acquired a kind of class. All these store fronts had different specializations, but each was a Fortunoff's.

Prosperity had finally arrived and Brownsville welcomed her with open arms.

9 — *Dem Bums, Foot-long Hot Dogs and the Loss of Innocence*

I have lived in Baltimore since 1977 after brief sojourns in Cleveland and Kansas City, all major league sports towns. While not a sports fan myself, I found it impossible to escape sports as news and conversation topic in such places.

The morning after the night the Baltimore Colts snuck out of town for Indianapolis, it was the dominant topic of conversation everywhere. Baltimoreans felt betrayed and they expressed it. Only I stood there, over morning coffee with my fellow workers and said, "Well, what did you expect? It's a business."

My lack of surprise dates back to another era - the rise and demise of The Brooklyn Dodgers.

The team had been part and parcel of Brooklyn identity under various names since the early 19th century and when Brooklyn became a borough on New Year's Day in 1898, the team became an object of pride, sharing honors with the Brooklyn Bridge itself. Before that final name stuck, the Brooklyn team had been called the Trolley Dodgers. Brooklyn was already known for the many trolley cars that crisscrossed around the borough. Being run over by a trolley is a nasty business, so perhaps being quick on one's feet, dodging these vehicles, equipped one for excellence on the baseball diamond. In any case, this monicker got shortened to the Brooklyn Dodgers.

When they did not perform up to expectations, they were called Bums by some. This term was immortalized in a cartoon and the nickname Dem Bums became part of the fan vocabulary.

Brooklyn loved its Bums, its Dodjahs, in huge disproportion to their win record. Loyalty to the Dodgers was a crucial part of Brooklyn's sense of identity and in this, Brownsville was no exception.

Ebbetts Field, where the Dodgers played their home games, was the mecca for fans young and old. My brothers, depending upon their financial resources at any one time would bike there, hike there, take the IRT subway and switch to the BMT - anything to cheer on the team. I am not a sports fan at all and recent attempts to explain football to me have failed miserably, but out of habit, I can visualize a baseball game from radio coverage alone. That's how much of it I had to endure. And when we got our TV set, Dodgers' games pre-empted anything else in our living room.

Ebbetts Field, mecca for Brownsville's loyal, diehard Dodgers fans was torn down in 1960 to make way for apartments. Talk about loyalty to the fans! It's a business, nothing more, nothing less.

Dodgers' games were written up in the sports pages of the papers every day and fans usually read the papers back to front, unless the team's activities made the front page. Dodgers' players were celebrities in their own right and made guest appearances at stores, especially those selling TV sets, banks and such.

They were treated as genuine heroes and thankfully behaved as such. You did not read about drug or alcohol scandals, hotel rapes - the players lived as far as we knew, as true role models. Their pictures appeared on the lids of ice cream cups, and as you licked off your favorite chocolate, vanilla, strawberry ice cream that had misted up the lid, you revealed a smiling face. Kids traded these lids like gold.

1947 seems to have been a watershed year on many levels. In baseball and especially in the history of the Dodgers, it was the year that the Dodgers broke the color barrier - the year of Jackie Robinson.

Brooklyn was proud of its Bums and Brownsville even more so. With its history of progressive politics, Brownsville's activists were thrilled with this step forward in civil rights. We all heartily embraced Jackie Robinson and were so proud of our team for having been the first. A year later, 1948, Harry Truman had tried to attach a civil rights plank to the party's platform and failed. But here was a concrete move that kept paying back - Robinson was a great player and his performance brought many Dodgers' victories.

Fans cheering as Dodgers win the big one.

There was a huge rivalry between the Dodgers and their subway adversaries, the NY Yankees and the Giants. The Yankees were damned strong adversaries and easily won pennants and World Series honors. Thus, victories over either of these teams would be all the sweeter. But somehow the farthest the Dodgers had gotten, was to win the Pennant - the World Series seemed forever out of reach.

It was such a long shot that one Brownsville deli, the Kishke King, sent out a promise it repeated year after year - if the Dodgers ever won the World Series, they would give out their signature foot-long hot dogs, FREE to all comers, no questions asked. This was for the most part, great marketing that didn't cost them a dime, and in the years in which the Dodgers did win the pennant and were in the running, it gave Kishke King great word of mouth advertising.

And then came 1955. The Dodgers found themselves winning the coveted pennant and they were again to be pitted against their arch rivals, the Yankees. The Dodgers were facing the enemy for the 6th time in 15 years and by the middle of game 7, it began to be apparent that the Brooklyn Dodgers were about to walk away with their first World Series - this was to be the year!!!!!

All those years of fan loyalty were about to pay off. Or were they?

For the moment, the owners of the Kishke King were scrambling to prepare for the biggest giveaway in Pitkin Avenue's history.

The Kishke King was Brownsville's answer to fast food. You bought your goodies to eat on the spot, note convenient trash can, or took it with you. In addition to burgers, hot dogs and such, you could also buy kishke (stuffed derma) by the slice or knishes stuffed with meat or potatoes.

What was the Kishke King, you ask? It was an early forerunner of fast-food, Brownsville style. Situated on Pitkin Avenue, in the less glamorous section, wrapped around Thatford Street, and through its window counter, they sold kosher hamburgers, hot dogs, kishke and knishes, French fries and cold drinks. In the summer you could also buy cold watermelon by the slice. Since most of its customers were pedestrian strollers and shoppers, it was not geared for car service as we know it today. You made your purchase and stood around eating it or strolled away with it. Others bought food there for take-home purposes.

Kishke King owned the building and the walls bore some of the most garish advertising around, more Coney Island carnival, than Pitkin Avenue elegance. And I am sure this day was never equaled for the owners of this establishment. True, they were giving away free foot-longs and buns, but the other items, including drinks, fries and other sides, were still being sold as well.

Sandy Koufax, a nice Jewish boy from Brownsville, at the World Series game.

Well, the day came and the word had definitely spread. Lines wound around the store for blocks and blocks as kids and grown-ups alike waited for hours for their freebies. Everyone was in great spirits. Dodger fans came from all over Brooklyn as well.

Subsequently, wrangling began over a new ballpark to replace Ebbetts Field. There was a half-hearted attempt to placate manager O'Malley by Mayor Wagner and a ball park in Queens was offered and rejected.

The Giants were already halfway out the door to San Francisco and Los Angeles offered a brand new ball park.

So it happened. In 1957, two years after their glorious victory and decades of loyal support, The Brooklyn Dodgers, formerly the Bridegrooms, the Brooklyns, the Robins, the Trolley Dodgers, left Brooklyn for greener pastures.

And it is true - Brooklyn has never been the same. The Mets came into being at Shea Stadium and developed their loyal fans.

But nothing like the identification of a place with a team had ever happened before or since - it was an identity.

And it became apparent to us in Brownsville that after all was said and done, sports was nothing more than a business like any other. And fans were merely ticket-buyers. Nothing more.

I understand that a new ballpark, KeySpan Park, has been set up in the Coney Island area, with a Class A affiliate team, the Cyclones, doing a creditable job as a minor league team affiliated with the New York Mets.

Fans come and cheer the team, eat the food, root for their favorites. It's a small-town experience for a borough that has grown exponentially since O'Malley absconded with the team in 1957. Brooklyn is big enough to secede from New York and become a full-fledged city.

I also hear rumors from time to time that Los Angeles is looking to sell the Dodgers.

Is it too much to hope that one day Brooklyn will buy back the Dodgers name, build a new Stadium in Brooklyn, maybe in Brownsville, and put things to right?

Now I am not a sports fan. I don't even like baseball. But if I have to be dragged there in my wheelchair, oxygen tank in tow, I will be at that opening game. And hopefully, it will be against the Yankees.

KeySpan Park, phooey!

Yes, the street I grew up on was named for Theodor Herzl, the founder of Zionism and the coincidence was not lost on me.

Theodor Herzl, an assimilated Jew from Budapest and later Vienna, was transformed by the famed Dreyfus Affair, which he was covering as a journalist. In fact, the Paris correspondent of the influential liberal Vienna newspaper Neue Freie Presse was none other than Theodor Herzl. When he heard mobs on the streets of Paris shouting "Death to the Jews", he became convinced that assimilation into European culture would not put an end to anti-Semitism.

While other Jews throughout history had yearned for a return to the ancient homeland, and some had even returned as individuals, mostly for religious reasons, it was Herzl who gave birth to the idea of political Zionism, of the creation of an internationally recognized Jewish State.
As he presaged,

*"In Basle I founded the Jewish state . . . Maybe in five years,
certainly in fifty, everyone will realize it."*

To this end, in 1897, he convened the first Zionist Congress in Basle, Switzerland. And remarkably, this led, across a bloody circuitous route ending in the Holocaust, only fifty years later, to the establishment of the independent State of Israel. The U.N. voted partition, creating a Jewish State, Israel, and an Arab State, Jordan in precisely 1947.

How did this event impact life in Brownsville? You can imagine. Emotions ran from joy and elation and a feeling of never-before-felt pride to the bittersweet realization of the catastrophe that had just preceded it.

Roster of votes for partition in the U.N. Harry S. Truman seals the deal for the new nation of Israel, Herzl's dream realized as per Herzl's prophetic words.

Zionist organizations of every flavor had long flourished, while other voices, that had in the past been cool to the Zionist dream, or even opposed to it, joined in the chorus of celebration. The Daily Forward's front page ran blue ink headlines, reflecting the colors of the new Israeli flag. (For decades the editorial policy had not been pro-Zionist.) People danced horas in the street.

Many young people had been members of Zionist youth groups where people gathered to learn Hebrew, Hebrew songs and dances. Some of the ideologies reflected the Socialist kibbutz ideal of collective work, living and sharing, and it was cool for American Jewish girls in these Zionist groups to wear their hair short, put away the lipstick and don men's shirts with rolled up sleeves over big denim skirts.

Most of the Jews in Brownsville were of Middle European origin, Ashkenazim, and the Hebrew they spoke or sang in prayer was the Ashkenazi version - but, the oy sound was now replaced by the oh sound, uhs became ahs, "s" sounds became "t" sounds. Boys just starting to learn for their Bar Mitzvahs were being taught the new pronunciation. This was because the decision in the new Israel had been taken to favor the Sephardic or Middle Eastern pronunciation. A whole new modern Israeli language was being born right before our ears. It was an outright rejection of the Yiddish dialects. Brownsville's Jews still davened the same old way, while the new crop of Bar Mitzvah boys began preparing in the new "modern" Sephardic Hebrew.

Hebrew got itself added to the curriculum at Thomas Jefferson High School and the teacher, Dr. Horowitz, had even authored a textbook and earned himself the job of Department Chairman. It was a language textbook organized like French, Spanish, German and to a certain degree, Latin. I didn't choose to take it, concentrating on French and Latin instead, because Hebrew had already been part of my studies in the Yiddish school. Although once the state was announced, the dialect we were being taught was switched midstream from Ashkenazi to Sephardic, leaving me a permanent victim of dialectical confusion.
Parades along Pitkin Avenue now also included the blue and white flag of Israel alongside the red, white and blue.

In our building on Theodor Herzl's own street, one young man chose to make "aliyah", the voyage of "going up" to the land of Israel. His name was Danny Cohen. The Cohens, of Roumanian extraction, were given to large quantities of garlic and Mrs. Cohen's roasts would perfume or contaminate the hallways before every Sabbath and Jewish holiday. Depending on your tolerance for garlic. They had two other children, an adopted daughter named Helen who worked in the children's store on our corner, later becoming a buyer in a Brooklyn department store. The youngest, Rhoda, was always adorned in Shirley Temple curls and a big bow to match her dress. We were all so proud of Danny, a medical student, who had the courage of becoming a pioneer.

But he must have missed the roasts and garlic of Herzl Street, because one day he returned, by now a doctor, married and with a young child. He left because the economy was so bad, everyone lived on salads and gvinah, cheese. And he had had enough of gvinah. I heard a few years later that he had become a big shot director at the World Health Organization.

Israel Bonds became the chic gift for Bar Mitzvahs, weddings and circumcisions. Trips to Israel were now a designation of choice for those who could afford it. A sea change had occurred throughout the Jewish world and as we approach Israel's 60th Anniversary, we need to take a look back at Brownsville Jewry, to understand the dynamics of its impact on Jewish identity. You now had the State of Israel to wrap yourself around instead of a prayer shawl - it was new, secular, cool and energetic.

For the largest number of inhabitants, Brownsville had been the American continuum of the Jewish shtetl of Eastern Europe. Whatever your politics or degree of religious observance, you lived, breathed and operated in a Jewish world, despite conflicting forces at work. Many residents were still from the Old Country and the sounds of Yiddish were everywhere. The first generation had become Yankee-ized and among some there was a disdain for the old ways, an embarrassment over those who did not look assimilated, or sound American or pick up on American sports, entertainments, values, etc.

The new generation, fluent in English and wise in the ways American institutions worked, often held the upper hand over their parents and challenged parental authority. Yiddish theater, film and radio soap operas made a tasty meal of these stories.

As for those who were super-observant or members of Chassidic sects, while some of them lived in our midst, most tended to live in neighborhoods like Crown Heights and Williamsburg. We tended to assume their number was going to diminish over time. These groups tended to be indifferent or even antagonistic to the new State, basing their identity as Jews, foursquare in the area of faith and observance.

Herzl's dream had offered the hope of a real solution to the Jewish people's problem. Since anti-semitism was inescapable, he reasoned, at least let there be a Jewish homeland, where Jews could live in safety, in their own land. He had not counted on that hatred being directed at the very survival of that State right from the get-go, or what it would do to future generations of Israelis faced with daily threats from Arab neighbors, how it would shape their world outlook and even Jewish identity.

Brownsville Jews did not flock in droves to the new Homeland.
Tough as conditions were, most were not in a hurry to trade in shopping on

Pitkin Avenue for struggling to survive on a kibbutz in the desert. They were not about to give up brisket for gvinah. Or abandon the Brooklyn Dodgers in their quest for the next pennant.

In general, Jewish identity becomes a compromise. We support Israel every way we can - bonds, rallies, songs, adding Modern Hebrew to Jewish school curricula - but we're staying home. Israel feeds our pride as Jews - no longer refugees, we are people with a State of our own. We do our Jewish religious thing in a modern, un-embarrassing way, when convenient.

This compromise becomes the nucleus of modern Jewish suburbia as we know it, with a few surprises. In the post-war era, Brownsville's Jews work their way up the economic and social ladder and move out, more and more of them to the suburbs, and later on to other states, especially Florida and California. Here this mix of support for Israel and perfunctory religious observance becomes the norm.

Yiddish is rapidly replaced by English in daily life and Hebrew as the language of choice in religious education. The ability to read (even without understanding) prayers and Biblical text is emphasized, although conversational Hebrew never replaces Yiddish in the marketplace. In fact, just as everyone was about to say Kaddish (the mourners prayer) for Yiddish, a whole new movement to revitalize it sprang up a decade or two later. And the very, very observant folks turned out to be very much alive and bouncing -- and with a propensity for large families -- someone forgot to do the math. Chassidic Jews have become a vital part of modern Jewry. They are still in Crown Heights, where the world headquarters of Lubavitch still stands, and will continue to spread out - maybe even one day back down Eastern Parkway to Brownsville?

Back to Herzl's dream. Did the founding of a Jewish State solve the problems faced by Jews? Only partially. It did give us a Homeland, an identity as a people among peoples. But not only did it not put an end to anti-Semitism, it gave the world new reasons to hate us. Jewish assimilation rates, due to intermarriage and other factors, are causing worry all across the Jewish spectrum.
Brownsville today is virtually empty of Jews. But not because they all stood up in a mass and made "aliyah" to Israel.

Sixty years is a wink of an eye in human history. Time will tell.

For those of us who experienced World War II growing up, there was a sense of unity - everyone knew who the good guys were, and who the bad guys were. On one side were Hitler, Tojo and Mussolini - on the other, just about everyone else. And in our youthful ignorance of what had transpired between the Western countries and the Soviet Union before the war, and what was going on under Stalin's roof, we thought of Stalin as one of the good guys. The moving scene we saw in the newsreels at the Loew's Pitkin of G.I. Joe embracing Ivan across the river, on the way to Berlin and on to victory, brought tears and cheers. At the newsstand on Strauss, corner Pitkin, on the front pages of newspapers from the Daily News to the Daily Worker, headlines were getting bigger and blacker and the sense of imminent victory was in the air.

Then it came and the war was over - the celebrations, the revelations of Nazi atrocities particularly against the Jews - and Brownsville being a mostly Jewish neighborhood, this was uppermost in our minds - unity predominated. Then suddenly, the tone changed and Stalin morphed into a villain and by March 5, 1946 Winston Churchill made his famous Iron Curtain speech, setting the Cold War in full gear. We could hardly catch our breath.

Anti-Communist feelings, merged with the fears of a possible nuclear confrontation, gave rise and support to the power of one Republican Senator, Joseph McCarthy, noted for making unsubstantiated claims that there were many Communist and Soviet spies and sympathizers lurking everywhere, in the Federal government, in the arts, education and of course, Hollywood. He rose to fame in 1950 with his famous "I have in my hands, a list, which, if revealed ..." speech, culminating in the Army-McCarthy hearings of 1954. There were accusations, open or implied, blacklistings, people selling each other out to avoid being tainted by the "sympathizer" brush, or worse. People lost their jobs. It was a fever all over the country.

And poor little Brownsville was caught in the vise.

The multi-party nature of this community was the first to suffer. Everyone felt the threat. Teachers became extra cautious, especially those who taught Civics, History, Geography and even Literature. Residents with non-mainstream, but non-Communist views, were always feeling watched, or compelled to prove they were not Communists. Street meetings still took place, but the outspokenness was dampened. A typical response I might hear while handing out a leaflet for an upcoming Norman Thomas appearance would be, "Why don't you go back to Russia where you came from?" Norman Thomas was the perennial Socialist Party candidate, implacable enemy of the Communists (and the feeling was mutual!) The son of a Presbyterian minister, who himself also became a minister, he was a lifelong champion of progressive causes. Unfortunately, he had also been an isolationist, supporting America First along with Lindbergh, until Pearl Harbor, when he changed this policy. History has been very kind to him. I attended his funeral alongside attendees like Mayor Lindsay, union leaders and other voices from all over the political spectrum. Today there is a High School in Manhattan that bears his name.

In the meantime, "duck and cover" drills replaced the wartime air raid drills in the schools as people wondered what to do if we were struck by a Soviet A-bomb.

Peculiar to this neighborhood, along with other Jewish communities was a totally different concern. Those Jews, who after surviving the Nazi Holocaust, found themselves living behind the now-expanded Iron Curtain, Hungary, Poland, Czechoslovakia, Yugoslavia, Russia, the Baltics and Ukraine, had relatives in the United States and neighborhoods like Brownsville still tried to find ways to get them food, parcels, money, or best of all, a way out.

This meant that the ties were not totally cut. Some of the organizations that tried to help included HIAS and the Joint, others turned out to be front organizations for Stalin, and connections with them could be harmful. One had to tread very carefully.

Some of the Jews who had remained behind in Stalin's camp included sincere Communists, who carried his propaganda forward to the West. Shlomo Michoels, a gifted Russian actor, also headed the Anti-Fascist Committee. He became one of Stalin's newest victims with a staged automobile accident as Stalin's anti-Jewish paranoia began to swing into full gear. Then followed the killing of the Jewish writers and poets. And finally, at the end of Stalin's Reign of Terror, came the so-called Jewish Doctor's plot, with its terrible blood bath, which was only interrupted by Stalin's death in 1953.

My father read the Yiddish papers religiously, still scanning for survivor names. In the Sunday rotogravure section of this paper, he found copies of anti-Semitic cartoons, featured in the Russian humor magazine, "Krokodil" (Crocodile) which were a chilling indication of State-sponsored anti-Semitism, again rearing its ugly head.

Mr. Spivack, the Communist boss painter, tried unsuccessfully to explain it away. We all now knew Stalin had been no better than Hitler.

The day to day dynamics of the average person in Brownsville was involved in taking advantage of the economic boom, of GI Bill benefits to buy homes or go back to college, ultimately to earn a real living and to leave Brownsville behind. Many moved to better neighborhoods in Brooklyn, Queens, the Bronx, Long Island. The mood was far more evasive and anti-political than ever before.

Then came the tragic Rosenberg affair, which touched every Jew in one or another way, whether super-religious or secular, to the center politically or far to the left.

I cannot think of the Rosenberg case without deep visceral sorrow.
Julius and Ethel Rosenberg were major casualties of the so-called McCarthy Era.
While the affair itself is and was controversial, the fact remains that their
harsh sentencing was a by-product of that inglorious era.

The day of execution hung like a dark cloud over Brownsville. Whatever else, in these dark days, before the leftover pain of the Holocaust would even begin to be healed, a Jewish mother and father were to be killed, and two Jewish boys would be orphaned.

Protests abounded. The boys marched with signs reading "Don't kill my Mommy and Daddy." Supporters in America and Europe came out in support of the Rosenbergs. There were paid radio broadcasts and the White House was deluged with pleas for mercy. Even the Pope spoke out to stay the hand of the executioners. But nothing availed.

Shortly after 8 p.m. on the Sabbath, in Sing-Sing Prison on June 19, 1953, it took place. The first fifty-seven second jolt of electricity failed to kill Ethel. She was re-strapped to the chair and given two more jolts before being pronounced dead. Ethel was the first woman executed by the United States Government since Mary Surratt was hanged for her role in the assassination of Abraham Lincoln.

The day of the funeral was even more personal, since it occurred in Brownsville at the I.J. Morris Funeral Home.

If your politics were inclined to the left, you felt they had been wrongly condemned and executed. If to the right, you felt the shame of their crime.

I have never forgotten the mixed feelings in Brownsville streets all through the trial period. You could cut the air with a knife on the night of the execution and the day of the funeral.

I recently found a copy of a poem written by Ethel Rosenberg to her sons six months before the execution, which I took with me to a talk by one of her surviving sons, Robert Meerpol, in 2004. They run the Rosenberg Foundation, dedicated to caring for child survivors of political activists around the world.

I reprint the poem here, without comment.

If We Die
By Ethel Rosenberg

*(written in the Death House at Sing Sing on
Jan. 24, 1953- six months before the executions.)*

You shall know, my sons, shall know
Why we leave the song unsung,
The book unread, the work undone
To rest beneath the sod.

Mourn no more, my sons, no more -
why the lies and smears were framed,
the tears we shed, the hurt we bore
to all shall be proclaimed.

Earth shall smile, my sons, shall smile
and green above our resting place
the killing end, the world rejoice
in brotherhood and peace.

Work and build, my sons, and build
a monument to love and joy,
to human worth, to faith we kept
for you, my sons, for you.

Others have been convicted for espionage - no one has ever been given the death sentence since.

The Cold War dragged on for decades - but from the beginning, Jewish Brownsville paid a price. The spirit of free and open debate was permanently chilled and people focused more on personal issues, jobs, family, and essentially moving up and out. In this they largely succeeded.

In my growing up years, until we got our first TV, radio was the dominant source of information and entertainment at home. There was a tremendous variety of programming available, from the important fireside chats of President Roosevelt to Yiddish soap operas.

On weekdays, while the kids were in school many housewives would tune in to the radio soaps of the period, Ma Perkins, Stella Dallas and other tearjerkers. The New York Times station, WQXR, with its classical and semi-classical sounds, soothed my mother as she washed laundry, bent over the bathtub.

Saturday mornings, before we left for the movies was kiddie time, with adventure programs like the Lone Ranger, Superman, Jack Armstrong, and others. Most were sponsored by cereals and offered prizes and membership clubs. My favorite in this segment was the ever popular "Let's Pretend", one of the most imaginative shows of the period.

You were carted off to the story of the week in some kind of outlandish vehicle like a magic pumpkin on wheels while a fine repertory cast of radio actors took you into a world of wonders.

This program was continuously sponsored by the makers of Cream of Wheat To this day I remember the jingle and the merry music that accompanied it:

"Cream of Wheat is so good to eat,
Yes, we have it every day.
We sing this song, it will make us strong
And it makes us shout hooray.
It's good for growing babies and grown-ups to eat.
For all the family's breakfast,
You can't beat Cream of Wheat.
It's way up in flavor (whooshing noise here)
It's way down in price.
It's puh-lenty smooooooth." (a low voice came in here)

Baseball game coverage was everywhere from early Spring throughout the World Series - you heard it on the streets, blaring from store front sound systems, from fire escapes and rooftops - a very definite recognizable sound texture of announcers and crowds cheering and booing. Even when you were not paying attention to the particulars, you had a sense of what was going on.

Radio, it is said, is theater of the mind. Still, the most difficult concept to translate into our timeframe is one of the most popular radio shows of all time - The Edgar Bergen and Charlie McCharlie McCarthy Show, with Edgar Bergen as the straight man and a cast of marionettes including the lovable Mortimer Snerd. You knew what they looked like from the movies and promotional photographs - Charlie with his formal attire and monacle, Mortimer with his bucktoothed country bumpkin airs, complete with freckles. Each puppet had a different musical intro, so you recognized their entry into the scene. Yet he could have produced it in the studio, for all one knew, just Edgar Bergen, the sound effects man and the music - he didn't really have to have the dummies with him. Yet these characters were firmly imprinted on the public mind - they were celebrities as much as any flesh and blood creature on the planet.

A number of comedians had half hour or full hour shows and drew large audiences. There was Bob Hope, Eddie Cantor, and Jack Benny, each with its own cast of characters and repeated gag lines. Each show also had a band and a singer. Bob Hope had Marilyn Maxwell, Eddie Cantor had Dinah Shore and Jack Benny had the Irish tenor Dennis Day who also played comic foil in his skits.

And they all brought in celebrity guests and they performed before live audiences. The laugh track had not yet been invented. Burns and Allen offered their own formula of couple humor with George Burns milking the laughs from deliciously dim Gracie. The acid-witted Fred Allen offered an entourage of characters with foreign and regional accents and peerless humor. The comedian-based shows also featured big bands with famous bandleaders and the top hits

There were sitcoms of a sort, Amos and Andy, The Bickersons with Don Ameche as well as soaps like One Man's Family. The sponsors of these continuing dramas as with the daytime versions were mostly soap products. So now, younger readers, you know the origin of the term soap operas. Jewish characters also became popular on American radio in the ongoing "Molly Goldberg" series which featured the serio-comic dwellers of a Bronx tenement and the soap about an inter-married couple "Abie's Irish Rose", both very popular in Brownsville living rooms.

Sunday mornings, my father would sit down at the kitchen table with beef and barley soup and leftover chicken, pickles and wine spritzer made by squeezing seltzer water into a glass with a little Manischevitz wine, all the while listening to the Forward Hour in Yiddish, a mix of news, commentary, drama and music. This was followed by the Good Health Seltzer hour, in Yiddish and English, which featured music and comedy in Yiddish and English and a running soap opera (call it a seltzer opera) whose plot dealt with the day to day angst in the lives of Jewish immigrants - it was called "Tsoris Ba Laytn", translated as "The Problems People Have". The arrogance and disrespect of the American-born children for their Yiddish-accented clueless parents was a running theme. Other Yiddish programs followed, but my father also tuned into the Italian and Greek programming that followed as well, as he was particularly fond of the Oriental sound.

Henry Sapoznik's excellent Yiddish Radio Project has helped find and make available the sounds of Yiddish radio of the period.

WEVD, the station that carried multi-lingual programming, named incidentally for the perennial Socialist presidential candidate Eugene Victor Debs, billed itself as the "station that speaks your language." Saturday evenings, dinnertime, Brownsville tables (except for the strict Sabbath observers) tuned in to the Yiddish news - this was especially important during the war and immediate post-war period. At that time we also heard Yiddish music programming featuring the tenor Seymour Rexite. His sponsor was Barbasol, a shaving product, and he himself would sing their jingle.

Saturday nights featured "The Lux Radio Theater", one-hour re-enactments of hit movies, read by its key performers on the air. It was sponsored by Lux Soap Flakes. And after that, we would hear "The Chicago Theater of the Air, put on by the Chicago Tribune, which performed cheery operettas for the most part and threw in a political radio editorial for extras.

News was also important on the radio and I remember sitting up almost all Election night in 1948 as the returns came in, bearing the results of the battle between Truman and Dewey. Dewey was for me as close as you could come to a villain (he even had a mustache that reminded me of Hitler) and I would not go to bed until I knew Dewey had been defeated. Many of the pundits of the time had expected an easy Dewey victory, and Truman had not been very popular with the Dixiecrats in the South, so there was fear he would not win because of his battle to put Civil Rights planks in the Democratic Party platform to which they had been violently opposed.

Brownsville, in addition to being a target of commercials for nationally known products from soaps and cereals to toothpaste, condensed milk, cigarettes and such, also picked up a large dose of Jewishly-oriented products from matzos and kosher wine to men's suits. Many of these had amusing jingles in a mix of Yiddish and English. Henry Sapoznik in his award-winning Yiddish Radio Project, has salvaged archival recordings of this period. The most well-known of these commercials was a mix of jingle and low comedy for Joe & Paul, suitmakers for men and boys.

This commercial became so popular, it passed into the folklore and even today, you will find people who grew up during this Yiddish radio heyday in New York, who remember snatches of it. Just say "Joe & Paul"and they'll jump right in - how many commercials today, could stand such a test of time?

Brownsville even had its own radio station of Yiddish program, one of extremely low wattage, I am sure.

Mystery and detective shows were also very popular in Brownsville. Our father was not a fan. Mostly they were weeknight programs, and after commuting to New York to the garment district, coping with work and subway and bus crowds, all he really wanted was a good dinner at the table with my mother, a little time of peace and quiet. My mother wisely made it a policy not to give him bad news until after dinner. She never greeted him at the door with bad news, as is so often done these days. By the time he came walking from the Pitkin Avenue bus up the street to our doorway, we had already been fed. So he would sit down to a hearty meal, complete with soup, appetizer, dessert (usually fruit compose) and a glass of wine spritzer. Then he would read his Yiddish papers and journals and go to bed. He would be getting up very early in the morning before us and be gone before we got up for school.

But we loved a mystery. We, being all five Siegel siblings and our mother. We particularly loved "Mr. District Attorney", the hero, his chief detective Harrington, his lady assistant, and their war on crime.

I still remember the intro, read by the chief figure himself:

Änd it shall be my duty as District Attorney, not only to prosecute to the limit of the law. Then there was a program called "The FBI in Peace and War", mostly about catching Nazi spies and their collaborators.

Unfortunately, our all-time favorite, came on Thursday nights at nine o-clock. That was rather late. We had done our homework for our regular school and for Jewish school, a double dose. The pots and dishes had been washed and put away. We had been washed and scrubbed and were in our pajamas for the night. And Daddy was in bed.

In that tiny apartment sound carried. So what to do? A solution was found, more or less. The furthest spot from Daddy's sleeping area was the boys' room. So all six of us would huddle on the bottom bunk bed and close the bedroom door. But this was not enough to let our weary father sleep.

The program was called "Suspense" and it was meant to be scary. So we finally worked out a way to have our cake and eat it. We would huddle together, every Thursday from 9:00 to 10:00 with a blanket over our heads and turn on a flashlight so it wouldn't be too scary. The sound was turned way down as low as possible and we entered the spooky world of suspense together. Sometimes, even with these precautions, he would call out in Yiddish, "Nideriger, nideriger!" which means "Lower, lower!"

I have always treasured this memory, as a metaphor for the family closeness we enjoyed at that time, and wish we could again be as close as that, our Father trying to sleep in the next door bedroom and the six of us, huddled like a mother cat and her five kittens, transported by the magic of old-time radio.

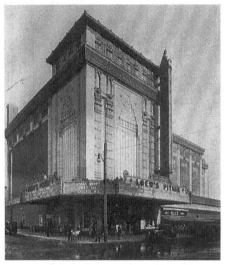

Let's start with the nuts and bolts. The dramatic Loew's Pitkin Theater on Pitkin Avenue between Legion Street and Saratoga Avenue, backed by East New York Avenue, was born on Saturday, November 23, 1929 precisely 11 A.M. Its seating capacity of 2,827 people included a big auditorium below, a sizeable upstairs balcony section and several loges. Designed by Thomas W. Lamb, it was one of the Loew's theater chain's highly touted atmospheric theaters, with a cloudy, starry sky and romantic lighting effects. There was a carpeted grand staircase in the lobby, with richly carved lion's head details. Even the restrooms were elegantly decorated with their own entrance lounge areas. The first movie at Loew's Pitkin was the talking-singing feature "So This Is College" (MGM) with Elliott Nugent, Robert Montgomery and Sally Starr. There was a stage revue as well, featuring performers direct from New York's Capitol Theater, comedians and comic acts, magicians, acrobats, musical artists and famed acts like Buck and Bubbles. This combo pattern continued for years and even when it was no longer the norm, there were occasional live vaudeville shows along with the films. At opening, it offered four De Luxe shows daily at 1:30-3:45-7:00-9:00. It was heralded as LOEW'S AMAZING NEW! PITKIN on Sat. Nov. 9, 1929 at 11 A.M.. Opening Day prices were 11 a.m.-1 p.m. .35 cents, 1-5 p.m. .50 cents, 5 p.m. to closing .75 cents. Note (Loges slightly higher.)

In its almost four-decade existence as a movie theater it played the top tier movies immediately after their New York movie house runs.

In addition to 5-act vaudeville shows, the programs also included the ever-present Henrietta Kamern at the organ, a Robert Morton classic pipe organ which was raised and lowered as needed. Henrietta accompanied the Follow the Bouncing Ball singalongs, and served up rollicking music at the beginning and end of major features.

Occasionally the theater featured Beauty Contests and eager younger movie-crazed girls would submit their photos which were displayed in the lobby. The concession stand served up drinks, large sized candy (including jumbo Tootsie Rolls, huge boxes of Nonpareils chocolate topped with white sugar pellets, and of course, freshly made popcorn.

Ushers were elegantly dressed good-looking young males and reportedly used this opportunity to meet and date young ladies of the neighborhood.

The building, with its Mayan inspired exterior was ringed on its Pitkin Avenue side with fine retail establishments. Today, the inside has collapsed but retail establishments of a lesser order still do business on the outer side of a fake wall.

These are the nuts and bolts. But in its heyday, in its glory, it was a whole lot more than the sum of its parts. The Loew's Pitkin was a pleasure palace, an escape from the struggles and humdrum existence of this working class neighborhood, its luxurious appointments and décor alone a sharp contrast to the squalor in which many lived.

Recent photos, prior to the collapse of the ceiling, show not only the vast size of the Loew's Pitkin, but the scenic magnificence of the surrounding sides. Henrietta and her beautifully stage-lit Robert Morton organ would emerge from the left front. And the orchestra pit was in front of the elaborate stage, in the center.

There was a Loew's Pitkin for everyone. For the reasonable price of admission, adults could enjoy at one sitting, top rung dramas, comedies, lavish MGM musicals, mysteries or westerns, paired with lower budget B pictures (some of which are now prized as "film noir" classics) along with the latest newsreels and, depending on the length of the main feature, additional short subjects. Everything about the experience, from the moment you came up Pitkin Avenue to the ticket booth, to your entrance, to the show itself was an escape. You walked on lush carpeting, sat in comfortable seats and enjoyed the best Hollywood could create.

This is a similar organ to the model played by Henrietta Kamern.

Our mother went to the movies by herself, either to the Pitkin or the Palace, usually on Tuesday nights, which were less crowded and management gave every lady a free dish. She loved the tearjerkers, especially the ones with Bette Davis most of all, and had found that having a good cry in the theater was very cathartic We developed a rating system for her. A really good one was a five-hankie picture. Two or one hankie pictures were disappointments. She would get dressed up, earrings and all, and put on a fancy hat for the occasion. It was normal to see our hard-working mother "all dolled up" for an evening at the movies by herself.

Saturday night was date night for young adults and teens. Unlike today, it was a time for dressing up, making up and showing off. Males wore shirts, ties and suits, adding dress coats with white silk scarves in winter. And it was cocktail dresses and fancy hairdos, jewelry and the whole nine yards for young ladies.

Couples in love spend the whole evening "making out" except for interruptions by the ushers. Couples not really in relationship spend the evening in a choreographed wrestling match. It goes something like this. He buys their first round of treats and they find their seat. He holds her seat for her, "like a gentleman". They settle in, make light conversation, nibble on sweets or popcorn and sip some Coke or Pepsi. The lights dim and the program begins. As the theater darkens and all eyes are on the screen, a male hand reaches for one or another part of the female anatomy. She knows what's happening and has three options. She can push the hand firmly away, leave it there passively but not respond, or jump right in there with him and "make out." If the hand is rejected, he tries blowing in her ear and looking soulfully into her eyes, especially in conjunction with a romantic portion of the movie.

The balconies were the places of choice for serious "making out" or heavy petting.

During breaks or scheduled intermissions, you went to the lavish restrooms, and combed your hair to be ready for the next round. Girls would re-do their make-up sitting at mirrors, surrounded by flattering lighting.
If a girl came by herself, and sat next to an empty seat, she would be easy prey for any unattached male who would sit down next to her. And the games would begin. Same choreography. The response was up to the girl. And if she really disliked the fellow and he didn't get the message, she would call the usher, to make him either vacate the seat or leave the theater.

The balcony section was popular for this sort of activity - in general the loges were too expensive, and the main section too out in the open.

The kiddie matinees on weekends were a whole different matter. If the main film was not considered appropriate for young eyes, or a hot kid movie was just released, that would be part of the double bill. A special section was roped off for kids and the aisles were heavily patrolled by searchlight-bearing ushers and matrons.

Kids would come in beginning with the opening of the doors around noon. They came with sandwiches, fruit and treats from home or enough money for the treats from the concession stand in the lobby.

Not only would the youngsters see a double feature and news, but also an array of short subjects, cartoons and that most popular kiddie favorite - the 12-part serial. Evolving from the Perils of Pauline type serial, they would pit a witless hero against equally witless villains. We called them, in Brownsville vernacular, the "chapters." There was a new chapter every weekend, ending in a cliffhanger, literally. Sets were unconvincing to any but young eyes. Kids cheered and booed and had a great time. The hero, The Phantom, or the heroine, Perils of Nyoka, would have found a secret entrance to a room on the way down the cliff, or a way to disarm the bomb that was about to go off. The intrepid Nyoka and her friends would be pitted against Vultura, Queen of the Desert, on a quest for the Golden Tablets of Hippocrates or some such treasure. And so on, to the 12th and final chapter. And then a new one would begin. The chapters kept the kids coming on a regular basis - no one wanted to miss finding out how the hero/heroine was rescued. On kiddie matinee days, there were huge signs at the movie house doors promoting the chapter and serial of the day. Each chapter had a dynamic name, presaging Indiana Jones, names not unlike The Temple of Doom, or Flaming Inferno, or Railway of Death.

Ah, the Perils of Nyoka - crushed by gorillas, about to be spiked to death in the shrinking room. Kids waited eagerly, week to week, to see how she would escape certain doom.

I am an incurable filmaholic and I watch Turner Classic Movies very often. So many of the films I see there or on other channels of that type, I first saw at the Pitkin, most of the 100 top films of all time. Casablanca, Best Years of Our Lives, Gone with the Wind, Goodbye Mr. Chips, Mrs. Miniver, Lost Horizon, all the MGM musicals. The Robert Mitchum film noir adventures. All the great comedies. The Pitkin was our eye on the world. Its newsreels shaped and ignited our patriotism in wartime.

It was more than that. It was a destination, and a place from which images flowed to inform, to entertain and to change thinking.

And for us, immigrants and the children of immigrants, caught up in our tight world of work and school, it was how we absorbed American ideas and values.

Even to this day, those who once lived in Brownsville speak with deep affection for this movie theater. I feel it is a shame that it has been allowed to deteriorate this far.

And I would suggest if anyone reading these pages has the money or the means or both to do something truly meaningful with it before there is any furtherdeterioration. I would imagine, in the light of the gentrification of Brownsville, that the building could be restored and converted into a museum of Brownsville's colorful turbulent history as a way station for different waves of immigration, while honoring the films that shaped two generations.

*Right hand page offers tickets to a Pitkin appearance in person of
The Three Stooges, in tandem with cartoons.*

If such a renovation were to come to fruition, it could revitalize Pitkin Avenue and make it a destination again.

Postscript: The fates of the lesser movie theaters in Brownsville and adjacent East New York. The Hopkinson Theatre, originally a live Yiddish theater and at one time a foreign film theater, was subsequently razed and is now a lot. The Stadium, where B mysteries like Charlie Chan were shown, met a similar fate and is now a small park. Loew's Palace, the Supreme, the Ambassador, the People's Cinema (nee Bluebird), the Livonia, The Lyric (Hendrix), Elite (Euclid), Kinema, Biltmore, Premier, Embassy, Warwick, Adelphi (Gem), Gotham, have ALL been demolished. Those that remain as churches include The Parkway, New Prospect (Ralph Ave.), the Montauk Arcade (Montauk) and Brair's Theatre (Powell) both on Pitkin Ave, the Penn, Sutter, Miller (Jehovah's Witness on site) all on Sutter Avenue.

In my Brownsville, parents were the voice of authority. But teachers, assistant principals and principals had the last word. Parents willingly surrendered traditional authority to the schools, because they believed, they knew in their guts, that only through education would their kids find a way out of poverty.

For a kid in trouble, there was no wriggle-room.

Discipline at home after a note from school, or a bad report card, could mean anything from being scolded, deprived of an allowance, grounded from the movies and even physical punishments such as spanking, slapping or worse, depending on the offense. None of this was considered abuse.

There was a lot of school in our lives. First there was the regular public school. There was no bussing, so everyone walked to school until High School - then you took public transportation which you paid for with a bus pass. The children of working mothers did not come home for lunch. Most of us walked back at noon to eat and then back for afternoon school.

When that was done, you came home for milk and cookies. And a load of homework. There was homework from every teacher, even the physical education department got in the act. Maybe you had time to play, but for many there was one or another form of Jewish school. Many youngsters also worked at after school jobs, running errands, helping storekeepers with stock.

The school authorities, in an attempt to fight juvenile delinquency, very tame behavior by today's standards, would open up the schools for athletic activities, after-school clubs and even optional separate religious instruction for Jews, Protestants and Catholics, with local religious teachers presiding. This way kids could get their dose of religious values without anyone offending anyone else. It wasn't such a bad idea, I think.

A lot of boys went to cheder or Hebrew School, mainly to prepare for their Bar Mitzvah confirmation ceremonies. Our neighborhood did not yet celebrate Bat-Mitzvas for girls, who instead got Sweet Sixteen parties. There were also a variety of religious day schools, the Beis Rivka for girls and yeshivas for boys. These were for the very observant.

In addition there were a number of after-school schools with a more secular and cultural orientation, usually reflecting the shade of political opinions of their parents. These schools taught Hebrew and/or Yiddish, Jewish history, labor history, Zionism, Jewish culture, songs and literature.

The devotion and idealism of these secular school Jewish teachers was remarkable. I attended a school sponsored by the Workman's Circle, a socialist-oriented organization and loved it. The focus was on Yiddish. and classes, five hours a week, were held in classrooms made from abandoned store fronts. You paid a few dollars a month in tuition and the rest was subsidized and supervised by a committee of volunteer parents. We gave concerts, did public recitations and dramatizations for special Jewish holidays. And of course, we all did homework. I completed all four years and graduated in a lovely ceremony at the store front school- my teacher was a gentle Yiddish poet named H. Maytin. Their high school, also a four year program, took place on the fifth floor of Washington Irving High School every Saturday and Sunday. Kids came from all over New York for two five-hour sessions, run exactly like a regular high school. The teachers were intellectuals and really opened worlds for me. The kids were exceptionally bright as well and two to four years older than I. And so at the ripe old age of eleven, I was traveling to Manhattan by bus and subway, on my own.

And of course, all of this extra schooling meant even more homework.

In my elementary school, P.S. 175, situated on Blake Avenue between Hopkinson Avenue and Bristol Street, twenty-five kids out of a class of thirty were Jewish, as were many of the teachers. We got all the Jewish holidays off. The remaining non-Jewish kids and teachers, had to go to school on those days, to skeleton classes - a waste of time and a source of resentment. I told them, as far as I was concerned, I didn't mind if the school closed down totally on those Jewish holidays. Miss Cherichetti, while a stern disciplinarian, shared her passion for making dolls out of clothespins, pipe cleaners and bits and pieces of cloth, tinsel, whatever, with the girls in the rapid advance classes. In later life, she traveled and collected dolls, donating her collection to a museum in Brooklyn.

Here's to you, Miss Cherichetti and the worlds your passion for dolls,
especially those in native costumes from around the world, opened up for me.

My Junior High was a totally different experience. It was like a time warp backwards. First of all, they split the boys and girls into two non co-educational schools. My brothers went to J.H.S. 66, which was pretty tough, but still a normal school. The school for girls, J.H.S. 84, on Glenmore Avenue, was conducted in an un-renovated building built back in the days of the Civil War. Classes were overcrowded and some rooms totally unusable.

The teachers were from the old school, mostly Irish spinsters and it was unusual to see a boy or man on the premises, except for the old man who served as building superintendent, a euphemism for janitor.

We had to dress in a kind of uniform, not exactly like the Catholic school uniform. Instead it consisted of a white middy blouse, although many girls substituted other, more stylish white blouses, a skirt - and a tie the color of your grade. The stated rationale was that this mitigated economic differences, and even if a girl owned just one blouse, she could wash it and iron it each day, and look just as good as her more affluent classmates.

Miss Vengashea taught 7th grade science like catechism. There was no probing or experimentation. She taught, in her Boston accent, "Whe-ah is ai-ah? (Where is air?)" And you had to answer as a class, "Air is everywhere." This was hardly conducive to building inquiring minds.

English was taught by Miss Lapham, also the school librarian, a gentle softspoken lady, from whom we learned to parse. For those deprived of this esoteric experience, parsing is breaking sentences into their parts of speech and diagramming their relationship to each other. It's like X-raying the language. Parsing has fallen out of favor. It ought to be brought back.

Math was taught by the tyrant of the school, Miss Dolan. Everyone feared her. She was about five feet tall, wore her hair in marcel waves and a bun, like Miss Grundy of the Archie cartoons. She was known to say in her strident high voice, "I may be small, but I'm mighty!"

I also took two language electives which I thoroughly enjoyed - French and Latin (more parsing here).

Gym was taught by a Miss Rubinstein under the name Hygiene and we all believed she wore the same ugly green gym suit she had started her career in thirty years ago. We all had to buy the same ugly green gym suit. Miss Rubinstein also taught a form of sex education which was naïve and innocent, if not totally laughable. We took notes and saw equally laughable sex education films that had no relevance to our lives and the action going on in the balcony of the Loew's Pitkin or club basements.

You got to Glenmore from my area by walking up Pitkin Avenue about twelve blocks and turning the corner, past the Mesivta Rabbi Chaim Berlin where pimpled adolescent religious boys in fedoras were studying Torah and Talmud. They were preparing for attendance at one of the excellent Yeshivas in New York. But come Springtime, they had more on their minds than learning - and would tease and whistle as the girls passed by. It was like running a gauntlet to get past them.

The population mix at J.H.S. 84 was radically different, half black and half white, and it was here, for the first time, that I interacted with black girls. My first moments were somewhat intimidating, not because of color, but because of size. You try being a stair monitor when you are 4 foot eight, and hordes of black girls, five foot five and taller, come chasing down the stairs at class break time. But bit by bit, individuals emerged, and we became friends. They were kinder to me than some of my cliquish Jewish classmates, many carryovers from P.S. 175, and this was the beginning of a lifetime of cordial interracial relationships for me.

The majority of Brownsville youngsters were funneled to Thomas Jefferson High in neighboring East New York, although some managed to attend the rival Samuel Tilden High. Those not interested in academic pursuits went to one or another vocational school. The specially gifted could try for Stuyvesant or Hunter High School.

Thomas Jefferson High, in its heyday, was a great high school with a remarkably high number of graduates going on to college. It was also strong in athletics, especially basketball. "Jeff" boasts a long celebrity roster of former students, some of whom were dropouts like Danny Kaye. When I started to work for the school magazine and sat down at the desk, someone told me that Shelley Winters had sat at the same desk.

The history of the birth of Israel is not complete without Mickey Marcus. Born David Marcus on Hester Street on the Lower East Side in 1901, he and his family moved to Brownsville when he was seven. There he excelled in a variety of sports and attended P.S. 109. He went to Boys High in 1919, then studied at CCNY for a year, before entering West Point. Upon graduation and the start of his military career, he also attended night classes at Brooklyn Law School, earning his L.L.B in 1927 and his Doctor of Law in 1928.

After resigning from the Army, Marcus married Emma Chaison, a Brooklyn girl, and built a career of public service as junior attorney in the Treasury Department, Assistant U.S. Attorney and Commissioner of Corrections of the City of New York under Mayor LaGuardia.

When World War II broke out, he re-entered the Army as a lieutenant colonel. Combining his law and military backgrounds, Mickey Marcus served as Judge Advocate, Provost Marshall and also served in the Army Civil Affairs Division. Promoted to the rank of Colonel in 1943, he contributed to the negotiations of several critical international agreements. On D-Day, with no paratrooper training, he parachuted into Normandy with the troops. He retired in 1947, having earned the Distinguished Service Cross, the Bronze Star, the Army Commendation Ribbon and the Order of the British Empire.

If you have seen the film "Cast a Giant Shadow" you have a sense of the role he played. In 1947, now in private Law practice, when the partition of Palestine into Arab and Jewish States was imminent, and the hostility of the Arab world inescapable, Mickey Marcus dropped everything to come to the aid of his brethren. He came to transform otherwise untrained, unorganized forces into a fighting army capable of defending itself against the expected Arab onslaught.

And when the attack came the day after Israel declared its independence, Israel was ready and Mickey Marcus went home.

But his work was not done. He returned to serve as supreme commander of the Israeli forces on the Jerusalem front. On June 10, 1948, just before the first Arab-Israeli truce, he was killed.

Said Israeli official Joseph Hamburger, "It is a fact that Colonel Marcus saved Jerusalem and you can imagine what Jerusalem means to us."

He is buried at West Point and Brooklyn has named a playground and a public school in his honor.

Brownsville seems a great place to be from. As it yearned and churned under the challenges of immigrant poverty, some just got by, others moved to a comfortable middle class lifestyle, some, like the Jewish gangsters of Murder, Inc. went wrong in the pursuit of money, and others went on to fame and fortune.

The most famous celebrity among Brownsville natives was the one and only David Daniel Kaminsky. I think of him as the Poster Boy for Brownsville. He came from nothing, and he made of himself a great name in the world.

The third and last son of a Jewish tailor from the Ukraine, he had the distinction of being the only Kaminsky son to be born in the United States. He was born in Brownsville on January 18, 1913 and attended P.S. 149. I remember a recording he made, imitating a child with a Brooklyn accent singing the "school song":

> *"One Four Nine is the school for me,*
> *Drives away all advoisity,*
> *Loyal and true,*
> *I'll be to you,*
> *Loyal, all, to 1-4-9*
> *Rah rah rah*
> *Lift on high the red and white*
> *Cheer it with all your might….."*

One-four-nine was the only school he ever formally completed. After that, like the majority of Brownsville kids, he attended Thomas Jefferson High in adjacent East New York. But he dropped out at age thirteen, to answer the call of show business. He ran away to Florida, where he began singing in the streets for money. There he changed his name to Danny Kaye. Next stop was the Catskills

Borscht Belt where he did radio work, then performing as a comic at various summer camps and hotels. A stint in the Orient followed and in 1938, at Camp Tamiment in the Poconos, he met comedy writer Sylvia Fine, who became his wife and the writer of some of his most famous materials. They produced one daughter, Dena, born December 1946. In 1939 he made his Broadway debut in "The Straw Hat Review" and later in "Lady in the Dark" by Moss Hart . The lead in "Let's Face It" with a Cole Porter score followed.

Through the early 40's. Danny did the night club circuit on Broadway and entertained American troops overseas during World War II. A brilliant Samuel Goldwyn movie career followed and a Command Performance before the Royal Family at London's Palladium. When his film popularity waned, he made a successful foray into television. He enjoyed a Broadway triumph as Noah in "Two by Two".

And then there was UNICEF, the United Nations Children's Fund which gave vent to his strong advocacy for social responsibility. As its representative, he was selected to accept the Nobel Prize for UNICEF in 1965. The Bnai Brith also honored his UNICEF work with a ceremony.

Danny Kaye conducted major symphony orchestras, raising millions of dollars for charity. In 1981 he received the Peabody Award and earned rave reviews as a survivor of Auschwitz in the television drama, "Skokie".

When he died of a heart attack in 1987, he was mourned by millions.
This native of Brownsville made it to the top, nationally and internationally. He was a brilliant comedian, fine actor, elegant song and dance man, one-of-a-kind mimic, gourmet chef, pilot, symphony conductor, UNICEF ambassador, husband and father and socially responsible human being.

Sandy Koufax was born Sanford Braun in Brownsville on December 30, 1935. During his career with the Brooklyn Dodgers and then the Los Angeles Dodgers, from 1955 to 1966, he racked up impressive statistics. He was named the National League's Most Valuable Player in 1963. He unanimously was voted the Cy Young Awards three times - 1963, 1965 and 1966, after having won the pitcher's triple crown leading both leagues all three seasons. At age 36, he became the youngest player ever elected to the Baseball Hall of Fame.

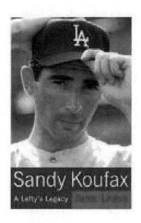

Sandy Koufax
A Lefty's Legacy

But his most significant claim to fame was not the statistics, not his wins, but a single act of courage. This left-hander was one of the few outstanding Jewish athletes of his time paying major professional sports. He had achieved much. Yet when, during the 1965 World Series, the day of the big game fell on Yom Kippur, the holiest day of the Jewish religious calendar, in which work is strictly prohibited, he chose not to play. Despite all kinds of pressures, he remained steadfast.

He was only a teenager when Dodgers owner Walter O'Malley proclaimed him "the Great Jewish Hope" of the Dodgers. But it wasn't until long after the team had abandoned Brooklyn that the man became the myth. Old-fashioned in his willingness to play, imbued in the Brownsville work ethic, he came through even when he was injured and so, it is remarkable that, despite his acute sense of responsibility to his team, Koutax answered to an authority higher than manager Walter Alston when he refused to play on Yom Kippur.

*How influential was this nice Jewish boy from Brownsville? Not only
did he inspire Martha Graham and Leonard Bernstein, and by extension
those who were in turn influenced by them, he lifted American themes
to new respectability in the world of music.*

Aaron Copland, the serious composer who integrated American folk themes with classical music, was born in Brownsville, New York, of Lithuanian Jewish descent. Before emigrating to the United States, Copland's father had anglicized his surname "Kaplan" to "Copland". Throughout his childhood, Copland and his family lived above his parents' Brownsville shop. Although his parents never encouraged or directly exposed him to music, at the age of fifteen he had already taken an interest in the subject, and aspired to be a composer. His musical education included time with Leopold Wolfsohn, Rubin Goldmark (who also taught George Gershwin), and Nadia Boulanger at the Fontainebleau School of Music in Paris from 1921 to 1924. He was awarded a Guggenheim in Fellowship in 1925, and again in 1926.

Copland defended the Communist Party USA during the 1936 presidential election. As a result he was later investigated by the FBI during the Red scare of the 1950s, and found himself blacklisted. Because of the political climate of that era, "A Lincoln Portrait" was withdrawn from the 1953 inaugural concert for President Eisenhower. That same year, Copland was called before Congress where he testified that he was never a Communist. Outraged by the accusations, many members of the musical community held up Copland's music as a banner of his patriotism. The investigations ceased in 1955, and were closed in 1975. Copland was never shown to have been a member of the Communist Party. Copland exerted a major influence on the compositional style of his friend and protege Leonard Bernstein, considered the finest conductor of Copland's works. Copland died of Alzheimer's disease and respiratory failure in North Tarrytown, New York on December 2, 1990.

Upon his return from his studies in Paris, he decided that he wanted to write works that were "American in character" and he first chose jazz as the American idiom. Several composers rejected the notion of writing music for the elite during the Depression, thus the common American folklore served as the basis for his work along with revival hymns, and cowboy and folk songs. His second period, the vernacular period, began about 1936 with "Billy the Kid" and "El Salón México". "Fanfare for the Common Man", perhaps Copland's most famous work, scored for brass and percussion, was written in 1942. It would later be used to open many Democratic National Conventions. The fanfare was also used as the main theme of the fourth movement of Copland's "Third Symphony".. The same year Copland wrote "A Lincoln Portrait" which became popular with a wider audience, strengthening in his association with American music.

*Martha Graham and Erich Hawkins starred in the premiere of
"Appalachian Spring " in 1944. The work was a nexus for two geniuses.*

He was commissioned to write a ballet, "Appalachian Spring", which he later arranged as a popular orchestral suite. The commission for Appalachian Spring came from Martha Graham, who had requested of Copland merely "music for an American ballet". Copland titled the piece "Music for Martha", having no idea of how she would use it on stage. Graham created a ballet she called "Appalachian Spring", which was an instant success, and the music acquired the same name. Copland was amused and delighted later in life when people would come up to him and say: "You were so right - it sounds exactly like spring in the Appalachians", as he had no particular program in mind while writing the music.

The ballet "Rodeo", a tale of a ranch wedding, written around the same time as Lincoln Portrait in 1942 is another enduring composition for Copland, and the "Hoe-Down" from the ballet is one of the most well-known compositions by any American composer, having been used numerous times in movies and on television. Copland was an important contributor to the genre of film music; his score for William Wyler's 1949 film, "The Heiress" won an Academy Award. Posthumously, his music was used for Spike Lee's 1998 film, "He Got Game", which featured a neighborhood basketball set to the music of "Hoe-Down". It is difficult to overestimate the influence Copland has had on film music. Virtually every composer who scored for western movies, particularly between 1940 and 1960, was shaped by the style Copland developed. Copland was awarded the Pulitzer Prize in composition for Appalachian Spring. In 2007, he was inducted into the Long Island Music Hall of Fame. He is also a recipient of the Phi Mu Alpha Sinfonia's distinguished Charles E. Lutton Man of Music Award for 1970.

Abe Stark, in a photo opportunity, sharing watermelon with a model.

Abe Stark, September 16, 1893 - July 1972, was an immigrant who, as a small boy, came to America from Russia with his parents, became a tailor and owned a men's clothing store at 1514 Pitkin Avenue in Brownsville. He also became a community activist, philanthropist, politician and eventually, a very popular Borough President (equivalent to Mayor or County Executive) of the Borough of Brooklyn.

A sign for Abe Stark's clothing store, placed directly under the Ebbets Field scoreboard in right-center field, told players "Hit Sign, Win Suit. Abe Stark. Brooklyn's Leading Clothier." Any player to hit the sign with a fly ball would get a free suit from Abe's store.

Due to the fielding of Brooklyn Dodgers right fielders Dixie Walker and Carl Furillo, Stark awarded very few suits. It has been said that, as long as the sign was up, the only opposing player to hit the sign on the fly was Mel Ott of the arch-rival New York Giants. What is known is that, upon the suggestion of a customer who pointed out how many free suits Furillo saved Stark from having to give, Stark gave Furillo a free suit. Stark became famous as a result of his sign, being seen first on movie newsreels and then on television.

He was very popular and rose through City politics to serve as President of the City Council from 1954 to 1962, and subsequently, as Borough President of Brooklyn from 1962 to 1970.

Being Jewish was what defined most of us who were born or grew up in Brownsville. Religious or not, American-born or immigrant, our Jewishness was a given - something in the air itself.

Our major exposure to the world of non-Jewish people and their cultures consisted in the main of what we saw in the movies, heard on the radio or jukebox or read in the press or library. A few of our teachers and school administrators were not Jewish. The major "others" included Blacks, Italians as well as some Irish, Russians, Poles and others of European origin.

For the Siegels at 38 Herzl Street, interaction with non-Jews began right in our own apartment building. The super and his wife, Mr. and Mrs. Becker, were Austrian immigrants. Upstairs, lived their daughter Tessie and her Irish husband Jack, their grandchildren Elizabeth, Ritchie and Barbara. Lizzie and I were casual friends and of the same age. But Ritchie and my brother Leybl (Louie) were buddies practically from the beginning, until Ritchie's untimely death of cancer - it was a true and close friendship.

The Harts, therefore, over the years, attended all our key family functions, birthday parties, graduations, marriages, bar mitzvahs, weddings and anniversaries. I babysat Lizzie's boy Billie from time to time. I understand from my brother that Billie is now a Barge Captain.

We visited the Harts and Beckers next door over Christmas and Easter and saw all their holiday decorations. During their holidays and Sundays, relatives would come, mainly to visit the Beckers, and go to church together. Mother would always have us bring up our holiday and Shabbes treats to the Harts, especially to Jack Hart, who loved Jewish ethnic foods like cholent, kugel, sweet and sour cabbage soup, kishke, and my mother's cakes.

Even this idyllic relationship had a few bumps. One notably, during the war years. I think Lizzie and I were about 8 years old, and we got into a squabble about something and it got physical. The two mothers stepped out into the street and had words and a little hair pulling - Tessie calling mother a "dirty Jew" and mother calling her a "Hitler". A period of not talking to each other followed, but this eventually eased and peace returned once more to 38 Herzl Street.

Blacks were definitely a visible minority, a whole group living in the tenements on East New York Avenue, the street that runs more or less parallel to Pitkin. In general they had the worst jobs, the worst housing and the lowest standard of living of all of us - they were the poorest of the poor. Drunken Stanley took it out by getting blind drunk and happy - I think he had a place to sleep in one of the basement apartments on Herzl Street. Another Herzl Street Black man was Mr. Baker. He also lived in a dark basement apartment and worked for a moving company. He had chronic foot problems and his feet were often wrapped. My father pooh-pooh'd racial slurs about Blacks (in Yiddish, "shvartse"), saying many times over, "I don't care if a man is green or purple. If he's a mentsh, he's ok in my book." And he would refer to Mr. Baker, poor but honest, hard-working and decent in every respect, as his example.

I used to play with a Black girl my age named Libby. We both liked to tell stories, making them up as we went along. She lived on East New York Avenue.

And for my brothers and their street games, there was no color line at all. They played with all the kids in the area - Jews, Blacks, Italians mainly. In addition to Ritchie, my brother Leibl used to run with a little Black kid named Brother (even his brother called him Brother, so that may have been his real name) and an Italian boy named Joey Labrano - they played together throughout their early years and into their teens, until High School.

There were very few Blacks in our elementary school, P.S. 175. But Junior High 84 was a totally different experience. It was an all-girls Junior High. Here, the population was split 50/50. There was a feeling of threat at first. There were so many, so suddenly, they were bigger and stronger and traveled in packs.

One day early in 7th grade, I found myself recruited as a staircase monitor. There I stood, at the second floor landing, trying to fulfill my stated mission of keeping everyone to the right and walking, not bounding down the stairs like a herd of buffalo. I was 4 feet 8 inches in my shoes, trying to control hordes of dark-skinned adolescent girls, closer to five foot eight, ready to challenge all authority, including mine as staircase monitor. A catastrophe of mis-casting by the teachers.

My first few days on patrol were terrifying. And then I found the key. I started to use funny voices, mimicking the cartoons. Soon everyone heard Donald Duck saying "Keep to the right." Their laughter broke the spell and I was able to do my job, while making friends at the same time. I credit this period of my life with opening up the humor valve in my personality, as I was pretty serious and bookish before that.

Politically Brownsville was very progressive and supportive of civil rights. Blacks and Jew worked together in community groups to try to improve our critical housing situation. It was a very natural, comfortable alliance. Jackie Robinson's barrier-breaking hire by the Brooklyn Dodgers was not only universally applauded, it was a source of pride.

Of course there were voices of prejudice within the Jewish community, usually among the less-educated. And these voices grew louder as old-time residents began to move up, and poor Blacks began to move in.

I cannot speak to the later periods of difficulty in

race relations, because by that time, my interests were elsewhere, working in mid-town Manhattan and going to CCNY at night. And then, leaving Brooklyn altogether.

There were some Italians scattered throughout the neighborhood, called "Talyener" in Yiddish, shortened version of Italyener. They were most visible in the form of the "black widows" who shopped on Pitkin Avenue. It seems, some-one explained, that someone who was widowed, wore black for the rest of her life. Most did not re-marry, no matter how young they were when their hus-bands died. The costume seemed to consist of shapeless black dresses, hair pulled back in buns, sometimes with a knitting needle sort of ornament or combs, black stockings and shoes. Black stockings being an item that needed frequent replacement, the stocking store around the corner, called Sultana, was a destination.

Freddy da Cop was Italian and relations were so close, that sometimes on a holi-day or day off, he would stop by, in civilian dress, with members of his family, wife, kids, others, just to chat amiably in the street. His retirement was a sad occasion for us.

Up until the mid-Fifties, when the neighborhood itself began to change, our experience of non-Jews occurred more through our leaving the boundaries of Brownsville, than any other way.

My Jewish High School, called Mitlshul, had classes at Washington Irving on weekends, so I learned from age eleven on to travel by subway all alone. The Automat where I ate lunch, the shops along 14th Street, all introduced me to the fact that New York was far from being all Jewish.

We as kids, did a whole lot of bus and subway traveling of our own - to muse-ums in Brooklyn, Manhattan and the Bronx, parks and zoos and other places of interest and amusement, where we encountered non-Jews and where we saw clearly, for the first time, that we were not in the majority.

Pitkin Avenue, being a commercial center, also reflected the larger American culture. Especially the chain stores. Despite being in a Jewish neighborhood, Brownsville's main shopping thoroughfare was all dressed up for the Christmas season with Santa Clauses and Season's Greetings on display in most of the shops.

The Woolworth's between Chester and Rockaway, the one with the gypsy fortune-telling machine outside, was festooned with lights, holiday trim, and sold all sorts of home and tree decorations. I was most fascinated by the multi-colored Noma lights, which looked like bubbling liquid - I could stare and stare at them.

And oh yes, there were a few gypsies around. Here and there, in an abandoned store, gypsies would set up shop. And sometimes families of gypsies could be seen strolling up the Avenue.

In general at this period, Brownsville's attitude to its non-Jewish co-residents was one of "Live and Let Live".

After the war, in the wake of the post-war boom, Brownsville's Jews began to move up and out. To Canarsie, Midwood, Boro Park, Queens and Long Island. And eventually to such far-flung places as Boca Raton, Florida and Los Angeles, California.

The Loew's Pitkin became a Black Church for a number of years. Then it was abandoned and fell into decay. The roof has come in, but there are still stores flourishing along its sturdy outer shell.

Blacks were not the last population in Brownsville. Next came the Puerto Ricans. And at this writing, the main population includes immigrants from Central America.

A final personal coincidence. I have lived in a modest house in a Baltimore sub-
urb for over thirty years now. The house directly across from me, was purchased
a few years ago by a family from Jamaica. But it turns out that prior to coming to
Baltimore, they lived in, of all places, Brownsville. In fact, they still have family
there, and visit Brownsville over many of the holidays. So my Brownsville con-
nection is not totally severed.

The long fought-for housing projects resulted in the tearing down of much of
my own street, Herzl between Pitkin and East New York, including the shul,
Ruderman's, Number 8 and the corner grocery store, but our building which
included Pitkin Avenue, in fact all the Pitkin Avenue frontage, still stands. 38
Herzl's corner store, on Pitkin, is now a Dominican grocery store. From aerial
photography, looking down on the building, I see clothing on a line, a sure sign
there are still families living there, just as we did.

As I google the area, I learn that gentrification is now taking place. In our time
we had turned to government sources to do something abut housing. Now, the
real estate developers have taken over, replacing old tenements and other housing with two-family dwellings that have backyards. Where do the poor people
go next?

This is the corner of Pitkin and Strauss. Same building is still extant, but such events happened here. The corner store was Shapiro's Delicatessen, that would close on Meatless Tuesdays during the war years. You could get some great sliced tongue here, or juicy franks called specials, plump and still attached to each other in rope-like fashion.. I can still smell those appetizing aromas. But up a few feet on Strauss, that's where the newsstand was. Yes, I can make out the hardware to which that newsstand was attached. In my mind's eye, I see it going full tilt, filled to overflowing with magazines and the latest news in at least four languages. Here I learned about the Battle of the Bulge, the Rosenberg executions, the fall of McCarthy from grace.

And in front, you could spend your change on chocolate covered jelly candies, Tootsie Rolls and fig newtons. At the side, you could buy ice cream mellow rolls and cones as well as ice cold Coke or Pepsi.

Where have they all gone, those denizens of Jewish Brownsville? The simplest answer is - most have gone to that great Jewish neighborhood in the sky. They are gone, dead and buried and except for the celebrities, largely unremembered except by their families.

The Jewish population came to Brownsville in ever-increasing waves, starting with the late 1890's. The last new wave of Jewish immigrants were the Holocaust refugees in the late Forties and early Fifties.

In between, Brownsville's Jewish residents were driven by several main goals, to survive, to educate their children for a better life and to get the hell out of Brownsville.

And in these goals they succeeded brilliantly. Carol Bell Ford in her book "The Girls" chronicles the role of Brownsville women and tracks a number of them, first to Canarsie and ultimately to Boca Raton. One of the girls in a candy store photo on the cover, I recognized immediately as Judith Goldstein, who had been in my classes from elementary school through junior high.

Brownsville "graduates" moved to better neighborhoods in Brooklyn, New York, the Bronx or Queens, or trekked out to Long Island. Others ventured farther afield. Some found jobs with the Federal government in Washington during the New Deal period. And stayed. Hardier souls traveled to California or Florida. One, my cousin by marriage, opened up an Indian Trading Post in Albuquerque, New Mexico. Some moved to Baltimore, Philadelphia or suburban New Jersey.

I have met people from Brownsville in the most unlikely places - I can usually tell them by their accents - more pronounced than a general Brooklyn accent. It takes one to know one.

Brownsville "graduates" of this era became teachers, administrators, business people, doctors, lawyers, politicians, community leaders and civil rights activists, rabbis and religious scholars, writers, performers (a lot of those), philanthropists. Others just got by and barely got out, leaving the rest to their more successful children and grandchildren.

Sad to say, there were also bad people in Brownsville, the most notorious being the members of Murder, Inc. In general, in my time, as others of the period will concur, Brownsville's criminal element did not impact our daily lives - we could sleep safely (even unattended children) on our fire escapes in the summer, leave windows and doors unlocked, walk the streets without hindrance even late at night.

There were no fly-by shootings, no drug dealers in the streets or schoolyards. Make no mistake, we were inner city poor in Brownsville. Many lived in cold water flats, with no heat. There were gangs, but if you were not in the gang, gang warfare did not touch you.

The apartments were small and crowded - the Siegels of 38 Herzl Street totalled 7 people and our apartment was only 3 tiny rooms and the kitchen. Our mother had to bend over the bathtub to wash our clothes with a scrubbing board, rinse, squeeze dry, re-wash, re-squeeze and hang the laundry out to dry on a clothes-line. This continued until the arrival of the first Laundromat in our neighbor-hood, when I was about eight or nine.

The Rubinsteins across the street had 12 children and were permanently on relief. Various Jewish charities and free loan societies helped people make it through their tough economic times.

We got out of Brownsville in stages, to schools of higher learning elsewhere in the city, to work in Manhattan, to GI Bill of Rights help for veterans seeking homes.

Even while we still lived there, we took busses, trolleys and subway trains to go elsewhere.

Top left, Utica Avenue station underground, gateway to the Outside World. Top right, Saratoga Avenue El platform. Downstairs were the Ambassador movie theater and Midnight Rose's candy store and unofficial headquarters of Murder Inc. Below, the Sutter Avenue/Rutland Road El platform.

Kids were often the recipients of free handouts of candy and toys at holiday times through a variety of organizations. There were cases of private philanthropy as well - our landlord, Mr. Feldman, sent several of us to a few weeks at summer camp, Camp Sussex in New Jersey.

Yet why is that when I run into someone from Brownsville, the very utterance of the name provokes a mutual sigh of yearning? We know something together that eludes words.

Having already published one small book on Brownsville, I still get e-mail inquiries from people wanting the book, for themselves, or for their parents or grandparents.

There is a pride these days in saying you are from Brownsville.

Some of this is perhaps due to the pride people feel in having come so far from the poverty they endured, pride in their own or the achievements of their fellow Brownsvillians in overcoming this poverty.

This is probably true and understandable. But there is something more at work.

We who grew up in Brownsville, immigrants, the children of immigrants, know in our deepest selves that Brownsville was far from a place of poverty - it was a place of enormous wealth.

Education, secular and religious, was placed on a pinnacle. School and homework were inescapable obligations and that respect was drilled into us in the home. What a foundation for success! Between school, homework, Hebrew school, more homework, a little play time, there was little time for kids to get into trouble. And when they needed more help, there were the waiting arms of after-school play groups, Scouts, Brownsville Boys Club. And kids were raised to be self-reliant - they went to school, Hebrew school and after-school activities on their own. The one and only Brownsville Children's Library was two floors of reading for all ages from beginners at the storybook level to budding adults. There was nothing worth reading you could not find there. You walked there by yourself and carried your own books.

Brownsville's treasure-house of great literature - here I moved from fairy tales to Dickens and Austen, read everything by Sabatini in systematic order - here, on the second floor, I read Karl Marx and discovered the study of linguistics. I would usually load up between ten and twenty books each week (after all, they were free) and begin reading them on the long walk home - oblivious of neighbors passing me. A library, all for and only for children - only in Brownsville.

There was no place you could hide if you chose to misbehave in public. Every block was like a community and many eyes peered from many windows. It didn't take long for the neighborhood grapevine to work and parents to learn what you had been up to.

Family values and the core values of the Jewish religion were at the heart of our Brownsville social fabric. Everyone, even the poorest, gave charity to someone needier. Neighbors did look after neighbors with whatever they had - a bowl of soup, a piece of kugel.

We all knew how to wrest beauty and spiritual riches from the most marginal settings. Sabbath and Jewish holidays had a magic of their own - somehow the poorest of the poor managed to find new or used outfits for the kids - to create a festive table and light the candles - and during these moments, we were rich as princes and princesses.

There seems to have been a shul on just about every street in Brownsville, some had more. They were not entities apart like today, but were integrated into the life of the street. Mourners heading towards the synagogue, carried on very dramatically, especially the women, with scenes of fainting not an uncommon occurrence.

Brownsville made us politically sharp and taught us how to think in a nuanced manner. We were not easy prey for sloganeering, not as kids, not as adults. But Brownsville also made us tolerant of differences, respectful of otherness.

Poko? Oh-Oh? Does this photo, taken November 2007, portend the demise of this grand old historic landmark? Say it isn't so.

And finally, I think, Brownsvillians share having lived together through the most trying yet most monumental moments of modern times -- the Depression, World Wars I and II, the unsettling Post-War Boom, the birth of the State of

Israel and the Cold War - all telescoped in a short span of time. From this cauldron came the true legacy of Brownsville, one of the poorest urban areas in America, yet also, arguably one of the richest.

JUICY APPENDICES
BROWNSVILLE HISTORY
(unidentified source, probably late 30's)

Brownsville extends from Ralph Avenue to Junius Street, between Liberty and Hegeman Avenues. With more than two hundred thousand people dwelling in its 2.19 square miles, it is the most densely populated district in Brooklyn. The population is predominantly Jewish. A group of Negroes lives on Rockaway Avenue, Thatford Avenue, Osborn Street between Livonia and Sutter Avenues. The only Moorish colony in New York is on Livonia Avenue between Rockaway and Stone Avenues. Italians live in the northern section of Brownsville; and on Thatford Avenue near Belmont is a small Arabian and Syrian quarter.

The main thoroughfare, Pitkin Avenue, named for John R. Pitkin, founder of the village of East New York, has large shops, a movie palace, and restaurants; great crowds of shoppers and strollers, day and evening, offer a colorful contrast to the numerous side streets with their dismal houses. The open-air pushcart market on Belmont Avenue, from Christopher Street to Rockaway Avenue, is the cynosure for local housewives, wives, who come to make thrifty purchases. Here Yiddish is the shopkeepers' tongue, and all the varieties of kosher foods, as well as delicacies particularly favored by Jews, are the leading articles of sale. In winter the hucksters bundle up in sweaters and stand around wood fires.

The area now called Brownsville, lying between the villages of East New York and Bushwick, was subdivided by Charles S. Brown in 1865. In 1883 there were 250 frame houses in the village. A group of East Side realtors in 1887 purchased land and erected many dwellings. They encouraged immigrants, chiefly Jews of East European origin, to move here from Manhattan's congested East Side. The extension of the Fulton Street el in 1889 and the IRT subway in 1920-22 made the district completely accessible from Manhattan, where many of the inhabitants work.

Old World customs dominate Brownsville life. There are more than seventy orthodox synagogues; the first, Beth Hamidrash Hagodal, at 337 Sackman Street, was organized in 1889. Numerous cheders, where young Jews receive instruction in orthodox traditions and customs, dot the neighborhood. On Friday night on Jewish holidays the streets of Brownsville are hushed. In all orthodox homes, after nightfall on the Sabbath eve, candles gleam, offering the only light in the room.

Numerous landsmanschaften, societies organized by immigrants from the same town or village in the Old World, supply most of the social life for the inhabitants. The landsmanschaften are also mutual benefit societies in which regular payments guarantee a doctor's service in case of illness, and a burial plot in case of death.

The building trades claim many Brownsville residents, and on Sunday morning, on the corner of Stone and Pitkin Avenues, carpenters, painters, electricians, and masons assemble to talk shop and find employment. Boss painters and contractors walk from group to group, picking their men. Behind the assembly rises a forlorn building, once a branch of the Bank of the United States, whose sensational bankruptcy in 1930 brought enormous losses to Brownsville residents.

Brownsville has always been hospitable to new social movements. From 1915 to 1921 this district elected Socialists to the New York State Assembly. In 1936 an American Labor Party candidate was elected to the Assembly, only to lose his seat in 1938. In 1916 Margaret Sanger established on Amboy Street the first birth control clinic in America.

BETSY HEAD PLAYGROUND_10.55 *acres*

This park is named for Betsy Head (1851-1907), a British immigrant who became a wealthy widow. Mrs. Head left the City of New York a bequest of $190,000 to build recreational facilities. She stipulated in her will that half of her residual estate should be given to sixteen charities, many of which were dedicated to the welfare of children, and the other half should be donated to the City of New York for the "purchase and improvement of grounds for the purposes of health and recreation." The land for Betsy Head Playground was paid for by the property owners of Brownsville at a cost of $250,000. The facilities of the playground were bought by the funds bequeathed by Mrs. Head.

Architect Henry B. Herts designed the new playground. It was built in 1915 by the Public Recreation Commission and turned over to the Parks Department later that year. The park included a rest pavilion, wading pool, playground, school farm garden, bath building, swimming pool, field house, running track, and tennis courts. It was one of the most complete and popular facilities of its time, embodying all the ideas current in recreation. A model of the playground was displayed at the Panama-Pacific International Exposition in San Francisco, and, according to the 1915 Parks Department Annual Report, "contributed greatly toward securing first prize for the New York City Parks exhibit."

In 1936 the park was extensively redesigned and the Olympic-sized swimming pool was constructed. Architect John Matthews Hatton's pool house exemplified the sleek Art Modern style with liberal use of glass block and a parasol roof. One of eleven pools built by the Works Progress Administration during the summer of 1936, the pool is a relic of the New Deal era. The construction project, organized by Parks Commissioner Robert Moses, and funded by the federal government, was part of a citywide effort to erect recreational facilities in under-served neighborhoods. The pools represented the forefront of design and technology. They attracted aspiring athletes and neighborhood children. The influence of the pools extended through entire communities, changing the way millions of New Yorkers spent their leisure time. Although damaged by fire soon after it opened, the pool was rebuilt in 1939.

Betsy Head Playground underwent a $5.2 million rehabilitation in 1983. The work included the reconstruction of the pool, ballfields, running track, and field event facilities. Also, new landscaping, benches, water fountains, an outdoor comfort station, curbing, trees, and shrubs contributed to the park. The multi-use facility endures as a model of park design.

LINCOLN TERRACE PARK_6.87 acres

This park is one of only two New York City parks named for our 16th president, Abraham Lincoln (1809-1865). Lincoln was born in a log cabin in Hardin County (now Larue County), Kentucky, and was mostly self-educated. He settled in New Salem, Illinois in 1831 and worked as a storekeeper, surveyor, and postmaster while studying law. In 1834 Lincoln was elected to the state legislature and in 1836 became a lawyer. Although he served in the House of Representatives as a Whig from 1847 to 1849, he lost two bids for the Senate in 1856 and 1858. Nonetheless Lincoln made an impression on his state and his nation over the course of his seven debates with Democratic opponent Stephen A. Douglas.

Lincoln successfully ran for president as a Republican in 1860. By his inauguration day in March 1861, seven southern states had seceded from the Union, and four more would follow in April. As the nation plunged into Civil War, Lincoln proved a skillful and thoughtful leader. In 1863 he issued the Emancipation Proclamation to free the slaves and delivered the Gettysburg address that eloquently memorialized fallen soldiers. He won re-election in 1864 against George B. McClellan. Five days after Confederate General Robert E. Lee's surrender on April 9, 1865, Lincoln was assassinated by John Wilkes Booth while attending a play at Ford's Theater in Washington, D.C. He died the next morning.

The City of Brooklyn purchased the first parcel for the 21-acre park between 1895 and 1897. The park was graded, planted with trees and shrubs, and enclosed with an iron fence. According to the 1918 Annual Report of the Brooklyn Department of Parks, anti-aircraft gun bases were installed in the park in "serviceable but inconspicuous locations" during World War I. Additional park parcels were acquired between 1916 and 1935. These included the northeast tip of the park, which had been acquired by the Department of Transportation as part of the IRT subway extension in 1916 and became parkland in 1928. The closing of President, Carroll, and Crown Streets between Rochester and Buffalo Avenues united the separate parts of the park.

Lincoln Terrace has long been a haven for the people of Brownsville and Crown Heights. Renowned authors Alfred Kazin and Elliott Willensky, who grew up nearby, remembered that the park was a favorite spot for hanging out and flirting. Yiddish-speaking residents knew it as "Kitzel Park" or "tickle park." In 1932 the Board of Aldermen named the west portion of the park for Arthur S. Somers (1866-1932), a local philanthropist and civic activist. Many of the park improvements, including tennis and handball courts, a playground and comfort station date to the 1930s.

The elegantly terraced tennis courts were reconstructed in 1996. The project provided new courts, retaining walls, fencing, benches, water fountains, security lighting, landscaping, and handicapped access. In addition to the courts, Lincoln Terrace offers wooded groves of gracious old trees, open lawns, two playgrounds, basketball and handball courts, a baseball field, and a comfort station.

This park is one of only two New York City parks named for our 16th president, Abraham Lincoln (1809-1865). Lincoln was born in a log cabin in Hardin County (now Larue County), Kentucky, and was mostly self-educated. He settled in New Salem, Illinois in 1831 and worked as a storekeeper, surveyor, and postmaster while studying law. In 1834 Lincoln was elected to the state legislature and in 1836 became a lawyer. Although he served in the House of Representatives as a Whig from 1847 to 1849, he lost two bids for the Senate in 1856 and 1858. Nonetheless Lincoln made an impression on his state and his nation over the course of his seven debates with Democratic opponent Stephen A. Douglas.

ZION PARK WAR MEMORIAL_Zion Park

This monument, also known as the Brownsville War Memorial, was sculpted by Charles Cary Rumsey (1879-1922) and dedicated in 1925.

In 1896, landowner Peter L. Vandeveer gave this property, bounded by Legion Street, and Pitkin and East New York Avenues at the junction of Eastern Parkway, to the City of Brooklyn. The "gore," so called for its triangular shape, took the name Vandeveer Park before being renamed Zion Park in 1911 by the Board of Aldermen, in acknowledgment of the large local Jewish community.

Alexander S. Drescher, chairman of the Citizens Memorial Committee and the Soldiers' and Sailors' Memorial Committees of the American Legion and Veterans of Foreign Wars (Local Boards 82 and 88), petitioned Brooklyn Borough Parks Commissioner John N. Harman to erect this monument in 1923. He also sought $5,000 worth of site improvements to accommodate the memorial. After delays in financing, the project went forward in 1925.

Architect Henry Beaumont Herts (1871-1933) designed the limestone stele and side pylons. The memorial committee procured Charles Cary Rumsey's services in 1921 to design two side reliefs of a soldier and sailor and the central motif of a stylized sword-bearing winged victory figure in low relief. The design also included carved Stars of David, and bronze honor rolls listing the names of servicemen from the community who gave their lives during World War I.

The sculptor Rumsey was born in Buffalo, New York, on August 29, 1879. In 1893, he traveled to Paris to study art. Upon returning, he enrolled at the Nichols School in Buffalo, graduating in 1898. He attended Harvard University, graduated in 1902, and in the same year studied at the Colarossi and Julien Academies in Paris, and the Boston School of Fine Arts. In 1906, he settled in Manhattan, and maintained a studio at 55 East 59th Street, soon showing his work in Architectural League and National Sculpture Society exhibitions.

In 1910, Rumsey married Mary Harriman (1881-1934) and continued his active artistic career. He had a particular fascination with animal art; in 1915, he exhibited an equestrian statue at the Panama-Pacific International Exposition at the World's Fair in San Francisco, and in 1916, his buffalo hunt frieze was installed on the Manhattan Bridge. In 1917, Rumsey helped organize the Sculptor's Gallery at East 40th Street in Manhattan. In 1920, he was commissioned to make the classical polychrome friezes for Rice Stadium (destroyed 1989). By 1921, he had completed a preliminary plaster and limestone version of Victory for Zion Park.

Tragically, Rumsey was killed in an automobile accident in 1922, before he had a chance to see his design to fruition. Edmondo Quattrochi, his primary studio assistant since 1911, finished the project. The completed work was dedicated November 1, 1925, by Brooklyn Borough President Joseph A. Guider (1870-1926), Brooklyn Parks Commissioner Edward T. O'Loughlin, and numerous local Jewish and veterans organizations. The sponsors noted, "The design itself does not alone symbolize the guaranteed freedom of our nation for the very names that will be inscribed upon it stand for toleration. The name of Sullivan will follow the name of Solomon, a Jew, a Catholic and a Protestant are recorded in one panel, a Negro's name is in juxtapostion to that of a white man."

Over time, the monument has suffered from weathering and vandalism, and the bronze honor rolls have been removed. In 1990, the monument was cleaned, the central bronze tablet reattached, and the inscriptions of the honor rolls incised into the side stone panels. The work was conducted through a $6,000 grant from the Mary Rumsey Foundation under the auspices of the Adopt-A-Monument Program, a joint venture of Parks, the Municipal Art Society and the New York City Art Commission.

Made in the USA
Las Vegas, NV
25 May 2021